# SURRENDERING TO SERENITY: LETTING GO OF CONTROL AND EMBRACING THE UNKNOWN

## CHRISTOPHER GARY

# CONTENTS

# DEDICATION

In honor of those navigating the intricate landscape of mental health, I dedicate these words to you. Mental well-being is not merely a journey but a sacred quest for inner peace and resilience. To those bravely facing the challenges of their mind, I extend my utmost respect and unwavering support.

In this pursuit, seeking guidance from a specialist becomes paramount. Therefore, I advocate for the utilization of authentic services tailored to address the nuances of mental health. Among these, Better Help | Professional Therapy with a Licensed Therapist stands as a beacon of hope and solace.

To every individual grappling with mental health conditions, know that you are not alone. Your journey is valid, and your struggles are acknowledged. May you find solace in the guidance of compassionate professionals who walk alongside you, offering insight, understanding, and a pathway towards healing.

This dedication is a testament to the resilience of the human spirit and the power of seeking help when needed. May it serve as a reminder that there is always a glimmer of light amidst the darkness, guiding you towards a brighter tomorrow.

# ACKNOWLEDGMENT

I extend my heartfelt gratitude to the one whose presence fills the pages of this book with warmth and inspiration—my soulmate.

Acknowledging you is more than a mere formality; it's an expression of profound appreciation for the love that permeates our shared journey. You are the quiet strength behind the words, the unwavering support in every chapter of life. To my soulmate, your encouragement and belief in this endeavor have been my guiding light. Your unwavering support has been the anchor that steadied me during the stormy seas of creation.

In all honesty, your love is the ink that colors the narrative of this journey, making it a testament to the beauty of shared dreams.

In the intricate dance of life, you are my perfect partner, and I couldn't have asked for more. This acknowledgment is a small tribute to the immense joy you've brought to my world and a whisper of gratitude for the love that makes every word, every sentiment, and every chapter richer.

With heartfelt appreciation,

**- AC**

# PREFACE

[Client will provide details]

# INTRODUCTION

Milestone birthdays often serve as beacons in the fog of our daily routines, illuminating the path we've traveled so far and casting shadows of doubt or pride on our journey. As we approach one, particularly those that end in a zero, a complex amalgamation of emotions begins to unfold, compelling us to pause and reflect on the chapters of our lives that have quietly slipped by.

As the calendar pages flutter closer to that significant date, a mixture of excitement and apprehension takes root. Why does this particular birthday feel different? Is it the societal emphasis on reaching a certain age or the personal expectations we set for ourselves years before? The reality is it's both. Society often marks these birthdays with heightened importance, engraining in us the notion that they are checkpoints for self-evaluation. Yet, our internal barometers measure success differently, comparing our present selves to the ambitious blueprints drafted in the naïveté of youth.

The eve of a milestone birthday prompts a deep, introspective journey. This is not about a fear of aging in the physical sense—though that may play its part—but rather an existential questioning of our achievements, relationships, and the disparity between our dreams and our realities. Have we reached the milestones we set for ourselves? Have we loved enough, given enough, and lived enough? This period of reflection is akin to standing at a crossroads, maps in hand, with roads leading in myriad directions. The past, with its successes and failures, lies behind us, tangible and unchangeable. The future stretches out, a blank canvas filled with potential but also uncertainty. In this moment of vulnerability, we question not only the decisions we've made but also the ones we're about to make. Are we pursuing what truly matters to us, or are we lost in the pursuit of what we believe should matter?

A milestone birthday is not just a time for solemn reflection; it is also an occasion for celebration. There is joy in having journeyed so far, in the friendships cultivated, the challenges overcome, and the simple fact of being alive. Yet, this joy is often tempered by a sense of nostalgia for the years gone by and a longing for the moments we didn't fully appreciate until they were past.

Amid these conflicting emotions, there is also gratitude. Gratitude for the lessons learned, for the people who have walked part of our journey with us, and for the opportunities that have shaped us. This gratitude serves as a gentle reminder that while we cannot change the past, we are the architects of our future.

The true essence of a milestone birthday lies not in the number itself but in the authenticity of the journey it symbolizes. Each person's path is uniquely their own, marked by a distinct set of experiences, choices, and lessons. In this realization, there is a liberation from the societal benchmarks of success and happiness.

The only true measure of our lives is the impact we have on others and the fulfillment we find in our pursuits. Falling short of our personal benchmarks often feels like a stumble in the marathon of life, a tangible reminder of our human imperfection. Yet, paradoxically, it is within these moments of perceived failure that the seeds of transformation are sown. This genesis of change, driven by introspection and the desire for self-improvement, marks the beginning of a profound journey towards realizing our potential.

## The Initial Discomfort

The initial realization that we've not met our own expectations can be jarring. It's akin to looking in the mirror and not recognizing the reflection staring back at us. This discomfort prompts a pivotal question: Why did we fall short? Was it a lack of effort and resources, or perhaps a misalignment of goals and values? This stage of self-questioning is uncomfortable but necessary, acting as the catalyst for a deeper exploration of our aspirations as well as actions.

## Acknowledging Vulnerability

Acknowledgment of our vulnerabilities is the first step towards transformation. It requires a certain bravery to admit, not only to ourselves but sometimes to others, that we are not where we wish to be. This vulnerability is not a sign of weakness but a testament to our strength. It's an acceptance that growth cannot occur without first recognizing the areas where we falter.

## The Importance of Reflection

Reflection is the cornerstone of self-improvement. It involves a deliberate and often challenging process of dissecting our failures, understanding our motivations, and critically assessing our actions. Reflection is not a passive act; it's an active, ongoing process that demands honesty and openness. What lessons can be learned from the shortfall? How can these lessons reshape our approach to our goals?

## Setting Realistic Benchmarks

One of the key insights from falling short is the realization that sometimes, our benchmarks are not aligned with our capabilities or circumstances. Setting realistic, achievable goals is not about lowering our standards but about understanding our limits and how to stretch them responsibly.

This recalibration of expectations does not mean compromising our ambitions but rather setting a pathway that is challenging yet achievable, allowing for incremental victories that fuel our motivation.

## Embracing the Journey of Self-improvement

Self-improvement is not a destination but a journey. It's a commitment to perpetual learning, adapting, and growing. This path is fraught with challenges, setbacks, and, yes, further instances of falling short. However, each of these moments is an opportunity for learning. Embracing this journey requires resilience, patience, and a positive mindset. The focus shifts from the end result to the growth experienced along the way.

## Transformative Actions

Transformation requires action. It's not enough to reflect on where we went wrong; we must take concrete steps to improve. This could mean acquiring new skills, seeking mentorship, or changing our approach to challenges. It involves experimenting with new strategies, stepping out of our comfort zones, and, most importantly, persisting despite the fear of failure.

## Cultivating a Growth Mindset

A growth mindset is pivotal in the genesis of transformation. It's the belief that our abilities and intelligence can be developed through dedication and hard work. This perspective encourages us to embrace challenges, persevere in the face of setbacks, and view failure not as evidence of unintelligence but as a heartening springboard for growth and for stretching our existing abilities.

As we embark on this journey of self-improvement, the transformation we undergo often has a ripple effect, impacting not just our personal and professional lives but also those around us. Our commitment to growth can inspire others, influence our relationships, and contribute to a culture of continuous improvement.

The act of narrating one's life story is an intimate and profound journey, a voyage that ventures beyond mere recounting of events, weaving through the threads of triumph, despair, growth, and revelation.

This process, steeped in vulnerability and honesty, serves as a powerful catalyst for catharsis, not only for the storyteller but also for the reader. Through the lens of personal narrative, we uncover the universal power of storytelling in healing, understanding, and connecting deeply with the human experience.

## Catharsis for the Storyteller

For the storyteller, the act of laying bare their life story is akin to opening a valve that releases the pressures of past experiences. This narrative process allows individuals to reframe and reinterpret their past, understanding their journey not as a series of disjointed events but as a cohesive and meaningful narrative. It is through this lens that pain, joy, failure, and success find their place within the broader aspect of one's life, offering insights and resolution.

The power of catharsis lies in its ability to transform silence into expression, converting the weight of unspoken stories into words that heal and liberate.

As storytellers articulate their experiences, they often encounter a profound sense of relief and clarity, as if the act of storytelling has provided a means to organize the chaos of life into something understandable and, therefore, more manageable.

## Healing Through Reflection

The reflective nature of storytelling encourages a deep dive into the self, prompting questions and revelations that might have remained unexplored otherwise. This introspection can lead to a greater understanding of one's actions, decisions, and their impacts, fostering a sense of self-compassion and forgiveness. The cathartic journey of recounting one's life story is not merely about revisiting the past but about redefining it, allowing the storyteller to claim ownership of their narrative and, in doing so, their healing.

## Catharsis for the Reader

The reader, on the other side of the story, engages in a parallel process of catharsis. Through the act of empathetic listening or reading, they partake in the emotional and psychological journey of the storyteller. This shared experience can be profoundly healing, as it underscores the universality of human emotions and experiences. The reader finds solace in knowing they are not alone in their struggles, joys, fears, and hopes.

Personal narratives often serve as mirrors, reflecting back the reader's own life experiences. This reflection can prompt readers to explore their own narratives, sparking a cycle of self-examination and understanding that mirrors the storyteller's journey.

In this shared space of vulnerability and authenticity, both the storyteller and the reader find common ground, a place where healing begins, and isolation ends.

## Building Connections

The telling of one's life story is a bridge built between the solitude of individual experience and the communal tapestry of human existence.

It is a reminder that, despite our unique journeys, we share common threads of emotions, challenges, and aspirations. This connection is healing, as it dismantles barriers of isolation and misunderstanding, fostering empathy, compassion, and a profound sense of belonging.

## Empowering Others

Beyond personal catharsis and healing, sharing one's life story has the power to inspire and empower others. Stories of overcoming adversity, transformation, and resilience serve as beacons of hope for those navigating their own challenges. They offer practical wisdom, insight, and the invaluable message that change and healing are possible. The act of narrating one's life story is a potent form of catharsis, offering a path to healing that is as varied and unique as the stories themselves. This process benefits not only the storyteller by providing a means to organize and understand their life but also the reader by offering connection, insight, and inspiration.

## The Journey from Anxiety to Serenity

In the heart of our fast-paced, turbulent world lies a profound quest for serenity—a sanctuary of peace that remains elusive to many. This book is dedicated to unraveling the path from the throes of anxiety to the embrace of tranquility, guiding readers through a transformative journey towards inner peace and acceptance. At its core, this journey is not about fleeing from life's inevitable challenges but about learning to navigate them with grace, understanding, and an open heart.

The essence of surrendering to serenity involves a deliberate shift in perspective, from resistance to acceptance, from turmoil to peace. Our journey begins at the source: Understanding anxiety not as the enemy but as a signpost, indicating areas within our lives that require attention and care. Anxiety often stems from our natural response to perceived threats, uncertainty, and the pressures of daily life. It manifests as a whisper of fear about the future, a relentless quest for control, and a barrier to experiencing the present moment. Recognizing this state as our starting point is crucial for mapping the transition to serenity. The path towards inner peace demands an embrace of vulnerability. Acknowledging our fears, uncertainties, and the aspects of life we cannot control is a powerful act of courage. Surrendering to serenity does not imply passive resignation but an active engagement with our inner landscape, exploring the depths of our emotions and the sources of our restlessness.

Central to our journey is the art of letting go—releasing the tight grip on expectations, outcomes, and the illusion of control. Letting go is a process of opening our hands and hearts to the flow of life and trusting in the unfolding of each moment. It involves a conscious decision to release the burdens we carry, from past regrets to future anxieties, allowing ourselves to move forward with lighter steps.

## Cultivating Mindfulness and Presence

Mindfulness and presence are the vehicles through which we travel from anxiety to serenity. By anchoring ourselves in the present moment, we learn to observe our thoughts and emotions without judgment. This practice illuminates the beauty of the now, teaching us to find peace in the simplicity of being rather than in the complexity of doing. Mindfulness cultivates an inner stillness, a sanctuary within that remains untouched by external chaos. Acceptance is the cornerstone of serenity. It is an acknowledgment of our current reality, coupled with the understanding that we have the power to choose our response to it. Acceptance does not mean giving up on change or improvement; rather, it's about recognizing that true peace begins with embracing life as it is, not as we wish it to be. This acceptance liberates us from the constant striving for a different reality, opening the door to genuine contentment and joy.

## Nurturing Compassion and Connection

Our transition to inner peace is deeply rooted in compassion— towards ourselves and others. Compassion softens our hearts, dissolves judgments, and fosters a sense of connection to those around us. It reminds us that we are not alone in our struggles and that our experiences are pieces in the intricate puzzle of human existence. Through compassion, we find solace in shared humanity, and in this connection, serenity blossoms.

As we navigate this journey, we discover that serenity is not a distant destination but a path we walk every day. It is found in the acceptance of imperfection, in the beauty of the present, and in the peace that comes from understanding that we are exactly where we need to be. Surrendering to serenity is an ongoing process, a choice we make moment by moment to live with open hearts and minds, embracing the full spectrum of our human experience. This book is an invitation to embark on this transformative journey, offering insights, practices, and reflections to guide you from the shadows of anxiety to the light of serenity. Together, we will explore the art of surrendering to the moment, to ourselves, and to the peace that resides within, waiting to be discovered.

# CHAPTER 1:
## THE MYTH OF PERFECTION

In an era where our perceptions are meticulously curated and served through the glossy screens of social media, the dichotomy between the virtual ideal and the tangible truth of our lives has never been starker. At fifty, standing at the precipice of reflection, the realization dawns - the vision of a life encased within a white picket fence, accompanied by the quintessential narratives of a perfect partner, child, and marriage, crumbles away to reveal a more profound, albeit unsettling truth.

## The Architectures of Illusion

Social media, the modern coliseum of validation, thrives on the spectacle of perfection. It's a world meticulously edited and filtered, where the mundane is glossed over for the highlight reel, creating a facade that glorifies an unattainable standard of living and being.

This digital mirage, while dazzling, fosters a culture of comparison where one's worth is measured against the staged achievements of others. The relentless pursuit of this digital validation and the pressure to live up to the societal benchmarks set by these illusions leaves many grappling with a sense of inadequacy and failure.

## The Unattainable Ideal

The myth of a perfect life - a stable career, a blissful family life, financial affluence, and eternal happiness - is a narrative sold to us not just by social media influencers but by movies, television, and advertisements. It's a compelling story, one that resonates with the innate human desire for stability and happiness. However, the reality is often a stark contrast. Life is an intricate tapestry of ups and downs; it's unpredictable and messy. The pressures to maintain the facade of a perfect existence can be suffocating, leading to a myriad of emotional and psychological struggles.

## The Crisis of the Midlife Reflection

At fifty, the reflection on what has been achieved versus the societal checklist of what *should* have been achieved can lead to a profound existential crisis. It's a juncture where the dreams of youth collide with the reality of adulthood. Once a symbol of success and stability, the white picket fence now feels like a reminder of what hasn't been achieved.

The perfect partner, child, and marriage - ideals heavily romanticized by society - when measured against the complexities of human relationships, often fall short, not due to a lack of love or effort but simply because perfection in human relationships is an illusion.

## The Liberation from Illusion

Recognizing the illusion does not diminish the achievements or the beauty of the imperfect, chaotic life one has led. Instead, it offers liberation, a chance to redefine success and happiness on one's own terms. It's a moment of reckoning, of understanding that the curated lives on social media are but a fraction of reality, often not showing the struggles, the failures, and the resilience it takes to move forward. The liberation comes from embracing imperfection, from finding joy in the real, unfiltered moments of life, and from the understanding that happiness is not a destination but a journey, replete with its own set of challenges and triumphs.

## Redefining Success

The true measure of success is deeply personal and cannot be quantified by societal standards. It lies in the strength to overcome adversity, the courage to pursue one's passions despite the fear of failure, and the ability to find contentment in the present moment. It's in the laughter shared with loved ones, the peace found in solitude, and the satisfaction of personal growth. Redefining success on these terms creates a foundation for a fulfilling life unshackled from the chains of societal expectations.

Perfectionism, often glorified as the relentless pursuit of excellence, has insidiously woven its way into the fabric of our society. This invisible thread, spun from the golden ideals of success, early retirement, and the quintessential white picket fence life, tugs persistently at the corners of our well-being, unraveling the tapestry of mental health with each pull. The narrative, amplified by social media, friends, and cultural norms, sings a siren song of a life where success is not just desired but expected. Yet, at fifty, confronted by the mirror of reality versus expectation, the reflection reveals not the promised utopia but a person grappling with anxiety, a sense of failure, and the haunting question: "Why can't I achieve perfection?" Perfectionism is not merely the desire to achieve excellence; it's an all-consuming drive where anything less than perfect is deemed unacceptable. It is a relentless taskmaster, constantly moving the goalposts, making satisfaction and contentment perpetually out of reach. This unyielding quest casts a long shadow over accomplishments, turning every achievement into just another stepping stone that isn't quite right, not quite enough. The pursuit of an unattainable standard becomes a Sisyphean task, where every effort, no matter how Herculean, feels insufficient.

# The Psychological Toll of Perfectionism

The psychological ramifications of this relentless pursuit are profound. Anxiety, a common bedfellow of perfectionism, gnaws at the mind, fueling a constant state of worry over the inability to meet these unrealistic standards.

This anxiety is not just a fleeting unease; it's a persistent dread, a foreboding that permeates every aspect of life, paralyzing decision-making and fostering a debilitating fear of failure. Depression, too, finds fertile ground in the soil of unmet expectations, where the disparity between aspiration and reality can lead to a deep sense of inadequacy and hopelessness.

# Perfectionism's Impact on Mental Health

The impact of perfectionism on mental health is a cumulative burden, a weight that grows heavier with each perceived shortcoming. It's a cycle where the fear of not being perfect exacerbates anxiety, which in turn impedes performance, further entrenching the sense of failure. This cycle can lead to serious mental health issues, including chronic stress, burnout, and even clinical depression. The irony is palpable: in the quest for a flawless life, one's mental health becomes the very flaw that perfectionism sought to eliminate.

# The Myth of Attainable Perfection

The core fallacy of perfectionism lies in the belief that perfection is attainable. This myth is perpetuated by societal norms and expectations, where success stories are polished to a sheen, omitting the trials, errors, and imperfections that are inherent to the human experience. The reality is starkly different; imperfection is not just a part of life—it's what defines our humanity. Embracing this truth can be liberating, allowing for the acceptance of flaws and failures not as signs of inadequacy but as opportunities for growth and learning.

# Navigating Away from Perfectionism

Navigating away from the clutches of perfectionism begins with redefining success. It requires a shift from external validation to internal satisfaction, from societal benchmarks to personal fulfillment. It involves setting realistic goals, practicing self-compassion, and valuing progress over perfection. This journey is not about lowering standards but recognizing that perfection is a mirage, a distraction from the meaningful, albeit imperfect, experiences that make life rich and rewarding.

At fifty, confronting the disillusionment of not having achieved a perceived societal ideal of perfection is a daunting but pivotal moment. It offers an opportunity to step off the treadmill of perfectionism and to reassess what truly matters. The cost of perfectionism is too high a price to pay, especially when it comes at the expense of mental health. By embracing imperfection, acknowledging vulnerabilities, and valuing the journey over the destination, one can find a path to genuine contentment, resilience, and a sense of accomplishment that no external standard of perfection could ever provide. The real success lies not in the attainment of perfection but in the courage to embrace life, with all its imperfections, and to live it fully and authentically.

Reflecting on whether five fingers, men, women, families, or individuals in their fifties are equal or should be on a perfect journey, I find myself confronting the heart of my struggle with perfectionism. This contemplation brings me to the sobering realization that the day I turned fifty was not just another birthday but a profound moment of reckoning. It was when I faced the stark contrast between the grand dreams of my twenties and the reality of my life. I had envisioned success and happiness, milestones I believed would naturally unfold with hard work and determination. Yet, here I am, married with a son, seemingly embodying the epitome of what one might desire, except for a nagging sense of underachievement.

The concept of perfection, I've come to understand, is as varied as the individuals who chase it. It's a subjective mirage, defined by the societal, cultural, and personal expectations that cloud our judgment. As I stand in the wake of my fiftieth year, I recognize that my journey has been uniquely mine, marked by its highs and lows, achievements, and failures. This acknowledgment brings with it a liberating, albeit challenging, realization: the beauty of life, and indeed, of ourselves, lies in our flaws and failures as much as in our successes. My twenties were a time of boundless optimism. I was a young dreamer who believed that by fifty, life's pieces would fall into a picturesque puzzle of success. However, the reality has been starkly different. Paths diverge, dreams evolve, and the unexpected becomes our reality. The divine comedy of life is that it seldom follows our meticulously laid plans. Yet, it's this very unpredictability that imbues our journey with richness and depth.

To answer the implicit question of whether life at fifty signifies the end or if there's more to strive for, I've come to a heartfelt conclusion: there is indeed more, much more than I once thought. My initial dreams, while not fully realized, have transformed, leading me to appreciate what I have and to yearn for what is still possible. The presence of my family, the love we share, and the collective experiences we've gathered are treasures that many seek but do not find, even by fifty.

The struggle with perfectionism is not just a personal battle; it's a universal dilemma. It demands of us to constantly measure our worth against often unattainable standards. The first step to dismantling this need for perfection is to acknowledge where I stand—not as an admission of defeat but as a starting point for growth. Turning fear into fuel involves a conscious decision to embrace vulnerability and to take positive action towards what truly matters.

Living with purpose and redefining success are not tasks that can be accomplished overnight. They require patience, resilience, and a willingness to forge a new path—one that values progress over perfection and personal fulfillment over external accolades. The journey ahead is about embracing my true self, with all its imperfections, and finding joy in the act of continual becoming. Letting go of the need to be perfect and moving towards embracing one's true self is a journey that begins with introspection and action. Here are the first steps articulated through the lens of self-love, acceptance, and the role of finances in the pursuit of happiness.

## 1. Practice Self-Love

The foundation of any significant change starts with self-love. Recognize your worth and value beyond accomplishments and material possessions. Self-love is about appreciating who you are at your core and treating yourself with kindness and respect. It means acknowledging your strengths and accepting your vulnerabilities. Celebrate your successes, however small, and be compassionate towards yourself in moments of failure or doubt.

## 2. Admit Where You Are

Honesty with oneself is a critical step in moving away from perfectionism. Take stock of your current situation, acknowledging both the good and the challenging aspects without judgment. Admitting where you are serves as a grounding point, a reality check that paves the way for setting realistic expectations and goals for yourself. This acceptance can liberate you from the chains of unrealized ideals and help you chart a course that aligns more closely with your true aspirations.

## 3. Live Life to the Fullest

Embrace the present moment and commit to living life fully. This doesn't mean pursuing every whim but rather engaging deeply with your current experiences and finding joy and fulfillment in them. Make the most of the relationships and opportunities you have now, and remain open to new experiences that can enrich your life in unexpected ways. Living life to the fullest involves a balance between striving for goals and appreciating the journey, including the detours and obstacles encountered along the way.

## The Role of Finances in Happiness

The relationship between money and happiness is complex. While financial security can provide comfort and open doors to experiences that bring joy, it is not a guarantee of happiness. Money is best viewed as a tool—a means to an end, not the end itself. It can facilitate the achievement of goals and provide for basic needs, which are foundational to well-being. However, the presence of wealth without meaningful personal relationships or a sense of purpose can lead to a feeling of emptiness.

People who find themselves with ample financial resources but lacking close, personal connections may still experience unhappiness. Conversely, those with strong familial ties and supportive relationships often report a high level of satisfaction with life, even in the absence of significant wealth. This suggests that while money can contribute to happiness by easing certain stresses and enabling certain experiences, the quality of our relationships and the pursuit of meaningful goals provide deeper, more lasting fulfillment.

The journey away from perfectionism towards embracing one's true self is personal and unique to each individual. It involves a blend of self-acceptance, mindfulness, and a reevaluation of what truly matters in life. Recognizing the role of finances as a tool rather than a measure of success can help prioritize personal growth, relationships, and experiences that genuinely contribute to happiness. As you embark on this path, remember that perfection is an illusion, and true contentment comes from living authentically and aligned with your values and aspirations.

# CHAPTER 2:
## EMBRACING IMPERFECTION

In the journey of life, the concept of imperfection often carries with it a negative connotation, seen as blemishes that mar the surface of our existence. However, when we delve deeper into the essence of what it means to be human, we discover that these imperfections are not merely detriments but are, in fact, integral threads woven into the fabric of our being. This chapter explores the inherent value of our flaws, arguing that they are what make us uniquely human, driving growth, fostering connections, and enhancing our capacity for empathy. It is a celebration of the beauty found in our imperfections, an expository and motivational narrative that invites readers to view their flaws through a lens of compassion and understanding.

## The Nature of Flaws

Flaws, by definition, are deviations from perfection. They are the mistakes we make, the insecurities we harbor, and the physical and emotional scars we carry. In a society that often champions ideals of perfection, flaws are frequently viewed as obstacles to success and happiness. Yet, this perspective overlooks the profound truth that it is our imperfections that render us beautifully human. Without them, the tapestry of humanity would lose its depth and texture, becoming a monotonous expanse devoid of individuality and resilience.

One of the most significant values of embracing our flaws lies in their capacity to foster personal growth. Each mistake we make, and every challenge we face due to our imperfections provides us with invaluable lessons that contribute to our development. The process of overcoming these obstacles not only strengthens our character but also enhances our problem-solving skills, making us more adaptable and resilient individuals. It is through confronting and accepting our flaws that we learn to push beyond our limits, exploring new horizons, and discovering our true potential.

## The Role of Vulnerability

Often perceived as a weakness, vulnerability is a powerful conduit for connection and empathy. By openly acknowledging our flaws, we invite others to do the same, creating a space where genuine relationships can flourish. This shared vulnerability fosters a sense of belonging and understanding as we realize imperfections are a universal human experience. In these moments of connection, we find solace in our shared humanity, drawing strength from the knowledge that we are not alone in our struggles.

## Flaws as Catalysts for Empathy

Empathy, the ability to understand and share the feelings of another, is greatly enhanced by our awareness of our own flaws. Recognizing our imperfections makes us more likely to approach others with kindness and compassion rather than judgment. This empathy bridges divides, builds communities, and fosters an environment where support and encouragement thrive. Through the lens of empathy, we see not the flaws of others as failings but as facets of their unique human journey deserving of acceptance and love.

## The Uniqueness of Imperfection

Our imperfections contribute to our uniqueness, making us who we are. They influence our perspectives, shape our choices, and color our experiences, creating a rich diversity of human expression. In a world of conformity, it is our flaws that set us apart, offering fresh viewpoints and innovative solutions. Celebrating this uniqueness encourages creativity and self-expression, allowing us to embrace our true selves without fear of judgment.

## Transforming Flaws into Strengths

Many of history's most influential figures have turned their perceived flaws into their greatest strengths. Dyslexia, once seen as a significant impediment, did not stop Albert Einstein, Leonardo da Vinci, or Pablo Picasso from reaching unparalleled heights in their respective fields. Their struggles contributed to their unique ways of thinking and creating, demonstrating that what may be considered a flaw in one context can become a formidable asset in another. This transformation is possible for each of us when we view our imperfections not as barriers but as opportunities for innovation and creativity.

Embracing our flaws requires a shift in perspective, one that moves away from the pursuit of unattainable perfection towards a celebration of our inherent imperfections. This does not mean resigning ourselves to our flaws but rather acknowledging them as an essential part of our growth and human experience. It involves practicing self-compassion and understanding that being flawed is not a sign of weakness but a testament to our resilience and adaptability.

## From Flaws to Features: A Transformative Journey

The journey of self-discovery and personal growth is often marked by a pivotal shift in perspective—a transformative realization that changes the way we view ourselves and our imperfections.

This shift from seeing our imperfections as flaws to recognizing them as features is a profound change that can dramatically impact our lives. It's a journey from a place of self-criticism and comparison to one of self-acceptance and uniqueness. Let's delve into this transformative process, exploring how such a shift occurs and the positive repercussions it brings.

For many, the journey begins at a point of frustration or despair, stemming from the relentless pursuit of perfection. It's a moment of realization that this pursuit is an unending race, one where satisfaction and self-acceptance remain perpetually out of reach. This acknowledgment often comes during times of vulnerability—when our perceived flaws seem most pronounced, and our spirit feels most diminished.

The catalyst for change might be an external event or an internal revelation, but its essence is the same: it challenges our long-held beliefs about the value of perfection and the nature of our imperfections. It could be the inspiring story of someone who turned their unique differences into sources of strength or perhaps a moment of unexpected acceptance from others despite our flaws. As we begin to question our perspective on imperfections, we start to see that our unique traits and experiences, even the flawed ones, add depth and richness to our character. They are the features that differentiate us, the brushstrokes in the portrait of who we are. This understanding is crucial in transforming our view of imperfections from negative flaws to positive features.

We learn that imperfections can foster growth, pushing us out of our comfort zones and challenging us to develop resilience and adaptability.

They also enhance empathy, as experiencing our own struggles makes us more understanding and compassionate towards others. Furthermore, our imperfections can encourage connection, creating bonds with others through shared vulnerabilities and truths.

## The Role of Self-Compassion

A significant element in this shift is the practice of self-compassion. Self-compassion involves treating ourselves with the same kindness, concern, and support we would offer a good friend in our situation. It means acknowledging our imperfections without harsh judgment and understanding that flaws are part of the shared human experience.

This compassionate approach helps to ease the self-criticism and negativity that often accompany our perceived flaws, facilitating a more positive and accepting self-view.

## Embracing Uniqueness

As we start to view our imperfections as features, we embrace our uniqueness. This doesn't imply that we stop striving for improvement but rather that we pursue growth to honor our individuality. It means recognizing that our unique blend of talents, quirks, and imperfections is what makes us who we are and that there's profound beauty and strength in that uniqueness.

## Impact on Life and Relationships

This shift in perspective has a far-reaching impact on various aspects of our lives. It alters the way we approach challenges, making us more resilient and open to learning from failures. It changes how we interact with others, promoting authenticity and deeper connections. And perhaps most importantly, it transforms our relationship with ourselves, leading to greater self-acceptance and happiness.

Building self-compassion is essential for fostering a healthy relationship with oneself, mitigating self-criticism, and embracing acceptance. Self-compassion involves treating ourselves with the same kindness, care, and understanding that we would offer a good friend.

This approach can significantly impact our mental and emotional well-being, leading to more positive life outcomes. Here are strategies to cultivate self-compassion, each designed to reinforce kindness towards oneself and alleviate the harshness of self-judgment.

### 1. Practice Mindfulness

Mindfulness is the foundation of self-compassion. It involves being present and fully engaged with the here and now without judgment. When you find yourself caught in a cycle of self-criticism, pause and observe your thoughts and feelings without identifying with them. Recognize that thoughts are merely thoughts; they do not define you. This detachment allows you to address your inner critic with understanding and patience.

### 2. Change the Self-Talk

The way we talk to ourselves significantly influences our self-perception. Start noticing the tone and content of your internal dialogue. Would you speak to someone you care about in the same way?

If the answer is no, it's time to consciously change how you talk to yourself. Replace critical or negative self-talk with words of encouragement and understanding. For instance, instead of thinking, "I'm such a failure," you could say, "I'm proud of myself for trying, and I learned something important for next time."

### 3. Write a Letter to Yourself

When you're feeling down or critical of yourself, try writing a letter to yourself from the perspective of a compassionate friend. What would this friend say about your situation? How would they lift you up and point out your strengths? This exercise can help you view your circumstances more objectively and kindly, encouraging a more compassionate self-perspective.

### 4. Practice Self-Care

Engaging in self-care is a tangible expression of self-compassion. It's about taking care of your physical, emotional, and mental health. This might mean setting aside time for relaxation, engaging in hobbies you enjoy, exercising, or simply ensuring you get enough sleep. By prioritizing your well-being, you send a powerful message to yourself about your worth and value.

### 5. Use Affirmations

Positive affirmations can reinforce a compassionate mindset. Choose affirmations that resonate with you and repeat them daily or whenever you notice your inner critic becoming loud. Examples include "I am worthy of love and kindness," "I am doing my best, and that is enough," or "I accept myself fully, with all my imperfections."

### 6. Seek Common Humanity

Remember that you are not alone in your struggles. Everyone faces challenges and experiences self-doubt at times. This understanding of common humanity is central to self-compassion. It helps to alleviate feelings of isolation and encourages a more accepting and kinder approach to dealing with personal shortcomings.

### 7. Forgiveness

Forgiving yourself is crucial for moving past mistakes and fostering self-compassion. Acknowledge your errors, learn from them, and then let them go. Holding onto guilt and regret only serves to deepen self-criticism and hinder growth. Remember, perfection is not the goal; learning and moving forward is.

### 8. Professional Support

Sometimes, developing self-compassion on your own can be challenging, especially if you're dealing with deep-seated issues of self-worth. Seeking the help of a therapist or counselor can provide you with the tools and support needed to cultivate a kinder relationship with yourself.

Embracing imperfections as milestones in our journey towards personal development and authenticity offers a refreshing and empowering perspective on growth. Rather than viewing flaws and failures as obstacles to our progress, we can see them as crucial steps that enrich our journey, making us more resilient, empathetic, and genuinely ourselves. This perspective shifts our focus from striving for an unattainable ideal to appreciating the beauty and lessons in the imperfections that define our humanity.

Every flaw we possess and every failure we experience carries with it a lesson waiting to be discovered. These lessons are the silver linings in our struggles, teaching us about resilience, patience, and the value of hard work. They remind us that growth often comes from discomfort and that progress is rarely a straight line. By viewing our imperfections as milestones, we learn to value the process of learning and evolving over the pursuit of perfection.

Viewing failures as milestones in our personal development teaches us resilience. It reinforces the idea that setbacks are not the end of the road but rather detours that lead to growth and new opportunities. This mindset helps us bounce back from failures with a stronger sense of purpose and determination, knowing that each setback is a step forward in our journey towards becoming our best selves. Our imperfections and the failures we experience also serve to deepen our capacity for empathy. They remind us that we are all human, navigating life's complexities with our unique challenges. This shared human experience allows us to connect with others on a deeper level, fostering relationships built on understanding and mutual respect.

Embracing imperfections as milestones reframes our pursuit of personal development. It shifts our goal from becoming perfect to becoming fully ourselves—flaws and all. This journey towards self-acceptance encourages us to set goals that align with our values and passions rather than external expectations. It inspires us to pursue what truly matters to us, making our lives more meaningful and fulfilling.

Our imperfections and failures are not just stumbling blocks but crucial steps on the path to personal development and authenticity. They are milestones that mark our progress, teach us valuable lessons, and make our journey uniquely ours. By embracing these aspects of ourselves, we cultivate resilience, authenticity, empathy, and a deeper appreciation for the beauty of the human experience. Let us then celebrate each imperfection and failure not as a mark of deficiency but as a testament to our ongoing growth and the authenticity of our journey.

# CHAPTER 3:
## THE POWER OF VULNERABILITY

In the journey of life, vulnerability often carries an unjust badge of weakness, a mark many of us strive to hide or eliminate. Yet, there's an emerging realization that vulnerability, when embraced, unveils not weakness but a profound strength and authenticity that can reshape our lives and relationships in ways previously unimagined.

## The Misunderstood Power of Vulnerability

Vulnerability is the emotional exposure that comes with being open to both experiences and relationships that could potentially lead to disappointment, pain, or criticism. It's the courage to be ourselves in a world that incessantly pressures us to conform to ideals of perfection. Far from being a liability, vulnerability is the bedrock of genuine connections, creativity, and growth. It's a sign that we are alive and fully engaged with the complexity of human emotions and experiences.

## Shifting Perspectives

The first step in redefining vulnerability is to shift our perspective. Rather than viewing it as a door to hurt and disappointment, we can see it as a bridge to deeper understanding and connection. This shift begins with self-compassion, recognizing that being vulnerable is not only natural but also a shared human condition. It involves acknowledging our fears, doubts, and imperfections and understanding that these do not define our worth or capabilities.

## The Strength in Openness

Opening ourselves to vulnerability paradoxically leads to strength. It's a strength that comes from confronting our fears, not in the absence of fear. When we allow ourselves to be vulnerable, we are taking a stand against the facade of perfection, choosing authenticity over pretense. This openness fosters resilience, as facing our fears and accepting our imperfections teach us that we can endure and grow from life's challenges.

## Authentic Connections

Vulnerability is the key to building deeper, more meaningful relationships. It invites others to see us as we truly are, imperfections and all, encouraging them to lower their guard and share their true selves in return. This mutual openness lays the foundation for relationships rooted in trust and understanding, where support and compassion flourish. Authentic connections like these enrich our lives, providing a sense of belonging and mutual care that is indispensable for our emotional well-being.

## Creativity and Innovation

Vulnerability is also at the heart of creativity and innovation. It involves the willingness to take risks to try new things despite the possibility of failure. Every creative endeavor starts with a leap into the unknown, a step outside of our comfort zones. By embracing vulnerability, we open ourselves to new ideas and possibilities, fostering an environment where innovation can thrive. It's in this space of uncertainty and openness that true creativity flourishes, leading to breakthroughs and discoveries.

## Overcoming the Fear

Overcoming the fear of vulnerability starts with small steps. It begins with being honest with ourselves and gradually extends to sharing our thoughts, feelings, and experiences with others. It requires patience and practice, as becoming comfortable with vulnerability is a process. It's also important to choose wisely whom we open up to, ensuring that it's someone who respects and values our openness.

## Embracing Vulnerability as a Lifestyle

Redefining vulnerability as a strength is more than a one-time act; it's a lifestyle. It means consistently choosing authenticity over safety and connection over isolation. It involves embracing the full spectrum of our human experience, with all its ups and downs. Living vulnerably is living courageously, constantly pushing against the boundaries of our comfort zones for the sake of growth, connection, and authenticity.

Redefining vulnerability from a position of weakness to a source of strength and authenticity is not only transformative but also essential for living a full and meaningful life. It challenges us to embrace our true selves, foster genuine connections, and engage with life in a more open and creative way. Vulnerability, with all its risks and uncertainties, is ultimately what makes life rich and rewarding. It's a reminder that the most beautiful aspects of life and love are often found not in moments of strength and certainty but in those of openness, risk, and authenticity. Creating genuine, deep connections with others is one of the most profound experiences in life, enriching our sense of belonging and understanding of the world and ourselves. At the heart of these connections lies vulnerability—an often misunderstood quality that, contrary to popular belief, is a powerful catalyst for fostering relationships marked by depth and authenticity. By embracing vulnerability, we not only invite others into our lives in a meaningful way but also embark on a journey of self-discovery and growth.

## The Essence of Vulnerability in Connections

Vulnerability is the courage to show up and be seen, to share our true selves, including our fears, desires, and imperfections. It requires a willingness to experience the full spectrum of human emotions—joy, love, sadness, fear—without hiding or masking our true feelings. This openness is daunting because it exposes us to the possibility of rejection or judgment. However, it is precisely this emotional risk that paves the way for deeper connections.

## Building Authentic Relationships

When we allow ourselves to be vulnerable, we signal to others that it is safe for them to be vulnerable in return. This mutual exchange of trust lays the foundation for authentic relationships. Sharing our struggles and successes, doubts, and dreams with another person and having them do the same creates a bond built on empathy and understanding. These relationships are characterized by a profound sense of connection and support, as both parties feel seen, heard, and valued for who they truly are.

## Vulnerability and Self-Understanding

The act of being vulnerable not only enhances our relationships with others but also deepens our understanding of ourselves. It compels us to confront our fears, insecurities, and the parts of ourselves we might prefer to ignore. This introspection can be challenging, but it is also incredibly rewarding. It allows us to explore the depth of our emotions, understand our reactions, and recognize our desires and needs. By facing our vulnerabilities, we gain clarity about our values, strengths, and arcas where we seek growth, leading to a more authentic and fulfilling life.

# The Power of Shared Experience

Vulnerability becomes a bridge to empathy, as sharing our own experiences opens the door for others to share theirs. This exchange fosters a sense of solidarity and understanding. Knowing that others have faced similar challenges or feelings can be incredibly comforting and reassuring. It diminishes feelings of isolation, reminding us that we are not alone in our experiences. Through this shared vulnerability, we can offer and receive support, advice, and compassion, strengthening the bonds between us.

# Embracing Vulnerability for Deeper Connections

To cultivate deeper, more meaningful relationships, we must embrace vulnerability with intentionality. This means actively choosing to share more of ourselves, listening deeply when others share, and approaching interactions with empathy and an open heart. It requires patience and practice, as becoming comfortable with vulnerability is a gradual process. However, the rewards are immeasurable—leading to richer, more connected lives.

Integrating vulnerability into our daily lives can significantly enhance personal growth, deepen relationships, and facilitate a journey of self-discovery and transformation. While the concept of being vulnerable might seem daunting, incorporating small, practical exercises into your routine can make vulnerability feel more accessible and manageable. Here are some exercises and tips designed to gently guide you towards a more open, authentic, and vulnerable self.

### 1. Journaling to Explore Your Inner World

Start a vulnerability journal. Dedicate a few minutes each day to write about your feelings, fears, desires, and dreams. This exercise is not about crafting perfect sentences but about honesty with yourself. Write about moments you felt vulnerable during the day, how it made you feel, and how you reacted. Journaling can help you understand your emotional triggers and patterns, offering insights into your inner world.

## 2. Sharing More with Trusted Friends or Family

Choose a trusted friend or family member and commit to sharing something personal with them each week that you might normally keep to yourself. This could be a fear, a dream, or an aspect of your life you usually don't talk about. The act of sharing and receiving support or understanding in return can reinforce the strength found in vulnerability.

## 3. Asking for Help When You Need It

Many of us struggle with asking for help, seeing it as a sign of weakness. However, acknowledging that we can't do everything alone is a powerful act of vulnerability. Start small by asking for help with minor tasks at work or home, and notice how it feels to open up and rely on others.

## 4. Engage in New Experiences

Stepping out of your comfort zone and trying new things naturally places you in a position of vulnerability. Sign up for a class, learn a new skill, or explore a new hobby that interests you. The key is to choose activities that challenge you, fostering growth and resilience.

## 5. Practice Saying "I Don't Know"

In situations where you're expected to have all the answers, practice the honesty of saying, "I don't know." This exercise challenges the pressure to always appear knowledgeable and perfect, encouraging authenticity and openness.

## 6. Mindfulness and Meditation

Engage in mindfulness practices or meditation focused on openness and acceptance. These practices can help you become more comfortable with your vulnerabilities by teaching you to observe your feelings without judgment, acknowledging them as part of the human experience.

## 7. Expressing Gratitude and Appreciation

Make it a habit to express gratitude and appreciation to the people in your life. Telling someone why they are important to you is a vulnerable act that strengthens bonds and fosters positive relationships. It encourages a culture of openness and sincerity.

## 8. Participate in Supportive Groups or Workshops

Join groups or workshops focused on personal development, where vulnerability is encouraged. Being in a supportive environment with like-minded individuals can make it easier to open up and share personal stories and challenges.

## 9. Self-Compassion Exercises

Practice self-compassion by treating yourself with the same kindness and understanding you would offer a good friend. When you notice self-critical thoughts, pause and reframe them in a more compassionate and understanding way. This practice fosters a healthier relationship with yourself, making it easier to be vulnerable with others.

## 10. Feedback and Reflection

Finally, actively seek constructive feedback and reflect on it openly in different areas of your life. Use this feedback as a tool for growth, acknowledging your imperfections and areas for improvement as opportunities to learn and evolve. Integrating vulnerability into everyday life is a gradual process that requires patience, practice, and courage. By incorporating these practical exercises into your routine, you can start to dismantle the walls you've built around your emotions, fostering a life marked by deeper connections, personal growth, and authentic living. Remember, vulnerability is not about weakness but about embracing the full spectrum of the human experience with courage and openness.

# CHAPTER 4:
## BREAKING FREE FROM OVERTHINKING

In a world where toughness and resilience are often heralded as virtues, admitting vulnerability might seem counterintuitive. Yet, embracing our vulnerabilities can be a profound source of strength and authenticity.

Let's dive into how transforming our understanding of vulnerability from a perceived weakness to a cornerstone of strength can revolutionize our personal and professional lives.

## Redefining Vulnerability

Traditionally, vulnerability is seen as a flaw—a chink in one's armor. However, this traditional view is not only outdated but also harmful. It discourages openness and authenticity, trapping many in a cycle of perpetual posturing and emotional isolation.

To redefine vulnerability, we must first accept that being vulnerable means being brave enough to face our true selves. It's about peeling back the layers of pretense and showing up as we are, not as we think we should be.

Imagine a world where leaders admit they don't have all the answers, where teams share their uncertainties and doubts, and where asking for help is a sign of strength. This is the kind of authentic engagement that redefining vulnerability can promote.

## The Strength in Authenticity

Why is vulnerability linked to strength? Because it demands courage. It involves stepping into the unknown, risking rejection and judgment, but also opening up opportunities for genuine connection and growth. When you're vulnerable, you invite others to see you as you are, imperfections and all. This builds trust and fosters deeper relationships—whether with friends, family, or colleagues.

In personal finance, one must confront uncomfortable truths to grow wealth and achieve financial independence. Similarly, in our personal lives, confronting emotional truths without pretense can lead to a richer, more authentic life.

## A Source of Empowerment

Vulnerability becomes empowering when it breaks down barriers. It helps us overcome the fear of judgment. Once you share your fears, failures, and uncertainties, you often find that others share those feelings, which can reduce feelings of isolation and boost collective morale. This can lead to innovative solutions and stronger teamwork in the workplace, as everyone feels safer expressing creative ideas and potential concerns without fear of ridicule.

Furthermore, embracing vulnerability can enhance leadership. A leader who admits their mistakes or acknowledges their flaws becomes more relatable and trustworthy. People are more likely to follow a leader who is human and fallible than one who is seemingly perfect but ultimately unapproachable.

## Vulnerability as a Learning Tool

Every time we allow ourselves to be vulnerable, we learn. We learn about our limits, our needs, and our strengths. We also learn about the compassion and capacity of those around us. Each act of vulnerability is an experiment in trust and adaptation. For instance, sharing a personal challenge with a colleague or superior can lead to support that might not have been forthcoming if you had chosen to struggle in silence.

Moreover, vulnerability is about letting go of control. In the financial world, Kiyosaki teaches that smart investors know they can't control the market, much like how, in life, we can't control everything. By acknowledging and embracing what we cannot control, we free up emotional resources to focus on what we can influence.

Vulnerability is not about weakness but the courage to be yourself in a world that constantly pressures you to conform to ideals of perfection and strength. By redefining vulnerability, we claim the power to be authentically ourselves, which is the ultimate form of strength. It leads to deeper connections, enhanced trust, and an empowering environment where people feel safe to share and innovate.

Vulnerability isn't just a buzzword—it's a cornerstone of building deep, meaningful relationships and a fundamental tool for understanding ourselves. When we talk about vulnerability, we often think of exposing our soft underbelly to potential threats. However, the real risk isn't in showing our true selves but in hiding who we truly are, not only from others but from ourselves.

## The Power of Authentic Connections

Think about the last time someone opened up to you in a raw and honest way. Chances are, that moment changed the dynamic of your relationship. It likely deepened your respect and trust for them. This is the power of vulnerability in action. When one person has the courage to be open, it often encourages others to do the same, creating a ripple effect that can transform relationships.

In the world of investing and business, where relationships are key to success, the principles are no different. A business partnership where each person knows the other's true intentions and weaknesses stands a better chance of weathering storms than one built on half-truths and guarded interactions. This same principle applies to personal relationships. When you're honest about your fears and failures, it not only lifts their burden but also invites others to support you and perhaps share their own.

## Understanding Yourself Through Vulnerability

Vulnerability also plays a crucial role in self-understanding. It's easy to think we know ourselves, but self-awareness requires peeling back layers, some of which we may have built as defenses against past hurts or failures. By confronting these layers—acknowledging and sharing them—we come to a clearer, more honest understanding of who we are, what drives us, and what holds us back.

Recognizing and admitting your financial fears—like the fear of losing money or the fear of not knowing enough—can lead to better financial decisions. The same is true for personal growth. Admitting you don't have all the answers can be the first step in learning more and improving yourself. Trust is the foundation of any strong relationship, whether it's personal or professional. And how do we build trust? Through consistent, truthful interactions. Vulnerability is at the heart of this. When people choose to share not just successes but also struggles, they demonstrate trust in others. In return, they are often met with empathy and understanding, which further cements the relationship.

For example, a leader who shares the challenges of a difficult decision or admits when they are wrong is more likely to inspire loyalty and trust in their team. People rally behind leaders who are not only strong but also human. They appreciate leaders who own their mistakes and view them as opportunities for group learning and improvement.

A crucial aspect of fostering vulnerability is creating an environment where it's safe to be open. This requires consistent effort to maintain a space where people feel protected against judgment and retribution. In such an environment, individuals are more likely to share their thoughts and feelings, contributing to a culture of openness and mutual support.

This principle can be applied in any setting—be it a corporate boardroom or a family living room. The key is to listen actively, respond empathetically, and withhold judgment, even when faced with admissions that are hard to hear. This not only strengthens bonds but also encourages a continual exchange of ideas and feelings, keeping the channels of communication open and active. Integrating vulnerability into everyday life can serve as a powerful tool for personal growth and transformation. To effectively harness the benefits of vulnerability, it's helpful to practice specific exercises that encourage openness and self-discovery. Here are practical tips and exercises designed to guide you in incorporating vulnerability into your daily routine:

### 1. Daily Reflection

Set aside time each day for reflection. This can be through journaling, meditation, or simply sitting quietly with your thoughts. Focus on what you felt during the day, especially moments when you felt defensive or uncomfortable. Reflect on what triggered those feelings. Writing down these reflections can help you process your emotions and identify areas where you might benefit from being more open.

### 2. Ask for Feedback

Regularly ask for feedback from people you trust. This could be professional feedback at work or personal feedback from friends or family. The key is to ask for honest opinions on specific situations or decisions. Listen actively without defending or justifying your actions. This exercise not only promotes vulnerability but also helps build stronger, more communicative relationships.

### 3.  Share Your Failures

Make it a habit to share your setbacks or failures with others. This could be sharing a lesson learned from a mistake at work or a personal challenge you're facing. By sharing, you normalize discussions about failures and setbacks, often seen as taboo or as signs of weakness. This fosters a culture of trust and mutual support, both in personal and professional spheres.

### 4.  Set Vulnerability Goals

Identify areas in your life where you feel you could be more open. Set specific, actionable goals to improve in these areas. For example, if you struggle to express emotions, a goal might be to tell someone how you really feel at least once a week. By setting goals, you make a tangible commitment to incorporating vulnerability into your life, which can lead to more meaningful interactions and personal growth.

### 5.  Practice Empathy

Empathy is closely tied to vulnerability. By striving to understand and share the feelings of others, you open yourself up to deeper connections. Practice empathy by actively listening to others without planning your response while they are speaking. Try to really feel what the other person is experiencing and reflect that understanding back to them.

### 6.  Challenge Your Comfort Zone

Regularly challenge yourself to step out of your comfort zone. This could be trying a new activity, initiating a conversation with a stranger, or tackling a project you find intimidating. Each of these challenges involves exposing yourself to the possibility of failure and judgment, which are key components of vulnerability.

### 7.   Engage in Supportive Relationships

Cultivate relationships where vulnerability is encouraged and reciprocated. Spend time with people who make you feel safe and supported. These relationships provide a foundation where vulnerability is seen as a strength, encouraging more open and honest interactions.

### 8.   Attend Workshops or Therapy

Consider participating in workshops or therapy that focus on emotional openness and vulnerability. Professional settings can provide structured opportunities to explore vulnerability in a safe environment, guided by experts trained to facilitate personal growth.

By integrating these practices into your daily life, you can begin to see vulnerability not as a liability but as a strength that enhances your ability to connect with others, understand yourself better, and grow as an individual. Each step towards vulnerability is a step towards a more authentic and fulfilling life. Remember, the journey of vulnerability is ongoing and evolving, and each small step can lead to significant transformations.

# CHAPTER 5:
## REWRITING YOUR INNER DIALOGUE

In the vast expanse of our minds, a quiet but dangerous enemy often lurks—negative self-talk. This internal adversary whispers doubts and fears, eroding confidence and impeding progress. Recognizing and confronting the detrimental impact of self-criticism is not just a necessity; it's an imperative for anyone seeking to lead a healthier, wealthier, and more fulfilling life.

Why do we listen to this internal critic? The answer lies in our natural, albeit misguided, mechanism to avoid pain and seek validation. We are wired to look out for threats and dangers, and this often extends to our perceptions of personal failure and inadequacy. However, this protective instinct can go awry, turning into a destructive loop of self-doubt and self-sabotage. What starts as a whisper can quickly become a shout, holding us back from pursuing opportunities and taking risks that are essential for growth.

The cost of negative self-talk is steep. It chips away at our mental health, placing us in a perpetual state of stress and anxiety. This psychological burden can manifest physically, affecting our energy levels, our ability to concentrate, and even our immune system's effectiveness. Emotionally, it traps us in a cycle of misery and self-pity, making it challenging to achieve or even set positive goals.

But how do we break free from this cycle? The process begins with awareness. We must become keen observers of our thoughts. Like a vigilant accountant scrutinizing a financial statement, we need to audit our internal dialogue. Identify the negative scripts that replay in your head—those statements that tell you you're not good enough, not smart enough, or doomed to fail. Acknowledge them, but do not accept them as truths. Instead, question their validity and confront their source.

The next step is to reframe these thoughts. In finance, a savvy investor turns a market downturn into an opportunity for growth. Similarly, we must learn to reframe our setbacks as opportunities for personal development. Instead of saying, "I always mess things up," one could say, "I've encountered a challenge, but I can use this experience to improve." This shift doesn't merely change the narrative; it changes the outcome.

Moreover, just as diversifying investments is crucial for managing financial risk, diversifying our sources of self-esteem is vital for emotional resilience. Do not let your sense of worth be dependent solely on one aspect of your life, whether it's your job, your relationships, or your appearance. Cultivate a broad sense of self that encompasses various facets of your identity and abilities.

It's also essential to surround yourself with positivity. Just as you would seek financial advice from experts, seek emotional and psychological support from those who uplift you. Build a network of friends, family, and perhaps a professional counselor who affirms your worth and encourages you to silence your inner critic. Their external voices can help drown out the negative chatter, reinforcing a more positive internal dialogue.

Confronting and overcoming negative self-talk is akin to turning around a failing business. It requires awareness, effort, and strategic thinking. It involves auditing your thoughts, reframing your mindset, diversifying your self-esteem sources, and surrounding yourself with positivity. This process is not just about stopping a habit; it's about starting a new journey towards a mentally healthier and emotionally richer life. By taking control of your internal dialogue, you empower yourself to take control of your life's direction—towards success, happiness, and fulfillment. Remember, the most crucial conversation you'll ever have is the one you have with yourself. Make it a positive one.

## Cultivating a Supportive Inner Voice: A Blueprint for a Positive Mindset

Many of us have experienced the harsh critic inside our heads. It's that voice that doubts, judges, and often stops us before we even start. But what if we could transform that critic into a coach? Imagine a voice that, instead of knocking you down, builds you up, encourages you, and cheers you on. This chapter explores how adopting practices that promote a supportive inner voice can significantly impact your approach to life and success.

The first step in fostering a positive mindset is to recognize the patterns of your current inner dialogue. Pay attention to the conversations you have with yourself during times of stress, decision-making, or failure. What tone does this voice take? Is it harsh, demeaning, or supportive? Being aware is akin to doing the groundwork before laying down a new investment strategy. You can't fix what you don't know.

Once you're aware of your internal dialogue, begin to intentionally shape it. This can be likened to choosing investments wisely. You want to invest in thoughts that yield high returns in confidence, motivation, and happiness. Start by reframing negative thoughts. For instance, replace thoughts like, "I can't handle this," with "I will do the best I can." This isn't just positive thinking—it's about giving yourself the same respect and encouragement you would offer a valued colleague.

Practicing gratitude is another powerful tool for cultivating a supportive inner voice. It shifts your focus from what's lacking to what's abundant in your life. Begin or end your day by acknowledging three things you are grateful for. This practice enhances your overall psychological resilience, making you less vulnerable to negativity. In financial terms, it's similar to having a diversified portfolio where the gains in one area can offset losses in another, maintaining an overall positive balance.

Mindfulness and meditation also play a significant role in nurturing a kind and supportive inner voice. These practices help you detach from the chaotic noise of the critic. Much like assessing a potential investment calmly and without bias, meditation allows you to observe your thoughts without getting entangled in them. It provides the mental clarity needed to choose responses that align with your goals and well-being.

Another critical practice is to engage in positive affirmations. These are powerful, concise statements that, when repeated often, reinforce the strength of your supportive inner voice. Affirmations like "I am capable and strong" or "I seize my opportunities" verbally reinforce your value and capabilities, similar to how regular investments bolster your financial standing over time. Furthermore, it's vital to surround yourself with people who reflect the voice you wish to adopt. Just as you would seek business partners who share your vision and drive, choosing a circle that echoes positivity, support, and encouragement is essential. The people around you can significantly influence your internal dialogue, so choose companions who uplift and inspire you.

Embrace challenges as opportunities for growth. This perspective is critical in developing a resilient, supportive inner voice. Each difficulty or failure is not a mark against your capabilities but a stepping stone to greater wisdom and strength. Just as an astute investor knows that the biggest risks often lead to the greatest rewards, viewing challenges through a lens of growth can transform your inner dialogue from one of criticism to one of encouragement and resilience.

Fostering a positive mindset through a supportive inner voice is crucial for both personal and financial success. It involves being mindful of your current self-talk, intentionally shaping it, practicing gratitude, engaging in mindfulness, repeating positive affirmations, choosing the right company, and viewing challenges as opportunities. These practices are not just about feeling better—they're about creating a foundation of thought that propels you towards your goals.

Daily practices for positive self-talk are crucial in cultivating a mindset that supports personal growth and happiness. Here are several practical exercises designed to replace negative thoughts with affirmations and encouragement:

1. **Morning Affirmations**: Begin your day by stating affirmations that foster positivity and strength. Stand in front of a mirror and declare affirmations like, "I am capable," "I am resilient," or "Today, I choose positivity." This exercise sets a positive tone for the day, charging you with confidence and a forward-thinking attitude.

2. **Gratitude Journaling**: Keep a gratitude journal and write down three things you are thankful for each day. This could be as simple as appreciating a good cup of coffee, acknowledging a productive work day, or cherishing a moment of laughter with a friend. Gratitude shifts your focus from what's lacking to what's abundant, significantly improving your mood and mindset.

3. **Mindful Breathing**: Throughout the day, take short breaks for mindful breathing exercises. Spend a few minutes focusing solely on your breath. This practice helps clear the mind, reduces stress, and creates a mental environment where positive thoughts can flourish. It serves as a reset button for your mind, especially when negative thoughts start to accumulate.

4. **Positive Thought Replacement**: Actively replace negative thoughts with positive ones. Each time you catch yourself thinking negatively, pause and reframe the thought positively. For example, change "I can't do this" to "I can learn how to do this with more effort and time." This exercise requires consistent effort but is highly effective in changing habitual thought patterns.

5. **Set Small, Achievable Goals**: Set daily, achievable goals and acknowledge yourself upon completion. These goals can be as simple as completing a workout, finishing a work assignment, or even organizing a small part of your home. Celebrating small wins builds confidence and reinforces a can-do attitude in your self-talk.

6. **Positive Visualization**: Spend a few minutes each day visualizing a positive outcome for your activities. Whether you are preparing for a meeting, planning a project, or approaching a personal goal, visualizing success can enhance your belief in your abilities and outcomes. This practice not only improves your mood but also prepares you mentally to succeed.

7. **Compliment Others**: Complimenting others boosts their morale and enhances your own. It shifts your focus from self-criticism to appreciating others, creating a positive feedback loop that enhances your own self-esteem and fosters a positive environment.

8. **Digital Detox**: Dedicate at least an hour before bed to unwind without digital devices. This helps reduce stress and prevents negative information from affecting your mood and thoughts before sleep. Instead, use this time for relaxing activities that promote calmness and positivity, such as reading a book, meditating, or planning the next day with a positive outlook.

By incorporating these exercises into your daily routine, you gradually transform your internal dialogue from negative to positive, fostering a supportive and encouraging mindset that benefits all aspects of your life.

# CHAPTER 6:
## LETTING GO OF CONTROL

In a world that relentlessly throws chaos at us like pies in an old slapstick comedy, it's not just natural but downright instinctive to try and take the reins on everything within reach. You know the feeling: if you can just manage your schedule down to the minute, orchestrate your relationships with the precision of a symphony, and juggle life's random lemons like a circus clown, then—*maybe then*—you can avoid getting hit in the face. But here's the reality, the cold, somewhat uncomfortable truth that most of us avoid like last year's expired milk: the control we think we have? It's about as substantial as a politician's promise before elections. It's an illusion, a comforting lie we tell ourselves because the alternative—that much of what happens to us is as predictable as a roulette wheel—is downright terrifying.

We hand you the ugly truth than a pretty lie and would be quick to point out that this illusion of control doesn't just mislead us; it royally screws us. It sets us up for massive frustration. It convinces us that failure is not just unacceptable but downright unnatural. It makes every unexpected twist in life feel like a personal slight from the universe when, really, it's just the universe being its chaotic, indifferent self.

So, what is this illusion of control exactly? It's a psychological quirk, rooted deep in our wiring, that convinces us we have a hand on the wheel when we're actually tied up in the trunk. It's believing that by worrying about every little detail, by planning and plotting and preventing, we can somehow outsmart life itself. We think if we strain hard enough, the universe will strain back. But here's the kicker: it won't. Take, for example, the gambler at the slot machine, throwing good money after bad with the ironclad belief that the next pull will be the big win. Or the stock market enthusiast who pours over charts and graphs to predict the next big crash or boom, as if the economy cares about their mortgage. These are not just quirks or hobbies; they are manifestations of the illusion of control. They believe they can predict and, therefore, control the outcomes of inherently unpredictable systems.

And what does all this controlling get us? Well, not much besides a good dose of anxiety and a chronic disappointment. When things inevitably don't go our way, the mental backflip we have to perform isn't just painful; it's disorienting. It shakes our foundation. We ask ourselves, "If I can't control this, what can I control?" Though we fight it tooth and nail, the answer is not a whole lot.

But, and here's a big 'but'—realizing that you're not in control can be liberating. It's like facing uncomfortable truths head-on that can free us from unnecessary stress and expectations. When you accept that control is a myth, you stop clinging to it. You stop setting yourself up for frustration. Instead, you start living in a way that's responsive, not reactive. You adapt, you adjust, and you accept that life's unpredictability is what makes it frustratingly beautiful.

Does this mean we should all just give up, sit back, and let life happen to us? Absolutely not. That's not the point. The point is to focus on what we truly can manage—our actions, our efforts, our attitudes. We can plan, sure, but we need to allow space for the unexpected. We can work towards goals, but we need to accept that sometimes the paths to these goals are more like suggestions than actual directions. We should think about control, like setting sails in the open sea. Sure, we can adjust the sails, but the sea will do what it will. Sometimes, it'll be smooth sailing, and other times, well, you better hold on because it's going to be a bumpy ride. The skill, the real trick to life, isn't about controlling the ocean—it's about learning to ride the waves.

Clinging to control is like clinging to smoke. It feels substantial, but let it squeeze through your fingers, and you'll find there's nothing there. By embracing life's inherent unpredictability and recognizing the limits of our control, we don't just become better equipped to handle life's inevitable storms. We also become better at enjoying the calm when it comes. We find that when we stop trying to control everything, we don't just cope with life better—we actually enjoy it more. So, maybe it's time to let go of the illusion, to stop grasping at air. Maybe it's time to just breathe.

## The Joy of Surrender: Embracing Life as It Is

In the relentless pursuit of personal and professional goals, the idea of surrender often gets a bad rap. We associate it with giving up, with failure, with not pushing hard enough. But what if I told you that there's profound strength and unexpected freedom in surrender? Not the white-flag kind of surrender you might be imagining, but a conscious acceptance of what is.

Let's break down the real joy of surrender—why accepting things as they are might just be the most liberating thing you can do for yourself.

## Why Surrender?

Picture this: you're in traffic and already late for an important meeting. You can feel the pulse at your temples, frustration mounting, stress accumulating. You're poised to explode. Now, consider this— what if you just accepted the traffic for what it is? This doesn't mean you're happy about it. It doesn't mean you don't wish things were different. It simply means you acknowledge the situation can't be changed at this moment.

The moment you accept the situation, something miraculous happens. Your stress levels drop, not because the external situation has changed but because your internal response has. This is surrender. And it's powerful.

## The Misunderstanding About Control

We love to feel in control. It gives us a sense of security and power. But this is largely a façade. Sure, you can decide what breakfast to eat or which shirt to wear. But there are far bigger things over which we have no control—like the weather, the economy, or the traffic.

Trying to control the uncontrollable is like trying to teach a cat to bark—it's futile and frustrating. In this context, surrender means understanding and accepting that some things are out of our hands. This acceptance doesn't make you powerless; rather, it redirects your energy from futile worry towards actions that you can actually influence.

## Surrender Is Not Passivity

It's important to clarify that surrender is not about passivity. It's an active choice. It involves recognizing the difference between what you can change and what you cannot. This is where surrender becomes a form of wisdom and strength.

In choosing to surrender, you're not being lazy or indifferent. You're making a strategic decision to accept the moment as it is, which, paradoxically, often gives you better clarity on how to move forward.

## The Liberation in Letting Go

The act of letting go can be incredibly freeing. It releases you from the burden of unnecessary expectations and the weight of unneeded pressure. It opens up a space where you can breathe, reassess, and navigate your life with a clearer vision.

When you stop fighting reality, you start living a life that's aligned with what actually is rather than what you insist it must be. This alignment brings a deep sense of peace and contentment. It's like being in sync with the rhythm of life itself.

## How to Practice Surrender

1. **Awareness**: The first step is always awareness. Recognize when you are resisting the reality of a situation.
2. **Assessment**: Ask yourself whether your control over the situation is real or perceived. More often than not, you'll find it's the latter.
3. **Acceptance**: Once you realize that you're wrestling with the inevitable, practice accepting it emotionally. This doesn't mean liking it—it means not letting it control your emotional state.
4. **Action**: Finally, redirect your energy. Focus on what you can do. Sometimes, the best action is to simply realign your attitude and expectations.

## The Ultimate Paradox

Here's the kicker—the more you surrender, the more empowered you become. It sounds counterintuitive, but it's true. When you stop expending energy on the uncontrollable, you conserve more energy for the things that truly matter. You become more effective, focused, and, ironically, more in control of your life.

Surrender isn't about giving up; it's about giving in to the flow of life. It's a strategic embrace of the realities that shape our existence, a recalibration of our innate desire to control everything. When practiced, surrender is not a sign of defeat but a sign of intelligence and strength.

It's the realization that sometimes, the best way to win is to stop fighting. This isn't just a nice sentiment—it's a practical strategy for a more peaceful, contented life. So, next time you find yourself clenching your fists in frustration, try opening your hands instead.

# Why Your Control Is an Illusion and How to Drop It Like It's Hot?

If you've ever felt the incessant urge to control everything around you, from the minute details of your daily routine to the grand trajectory of your career, you're not alone. But here's the kicker: this compulsion to steer every part of your existence is exhausting and mostly futile. Welcome to the art of letting go, a practice that isn't about indifference but about fostering a healthier, happier, and surprisingly more controlled life.

## The Illusion of Control

First, let's get one thing straight: the control you think you have? It's about as real as the nutrition in a pack of sugar-free gummy bears. We stress over traffic, weather, or whether our favorite team wins. But realistically, we have zero influence over these outcomes. The sooner you recognize that most things in life are outside your control, the sooner you can release unnecessary tension and focus on what genuinely matters.

## Why Letting Go Matters

Here's the deal: trying to control everything is like trying to staple water to a wall—it doesn't work, and it's pretty ridiculous. When you relinquish the urge to control, you open doors to new experiences, reduce stress and improve your overall well-being. It's about shifting from a mindset of "I must handle everything" to "I will handle what I can and adapt to what I can't."

### Step 1: Identify Your Control Triggers

Start by pinpointing what triggers your control freak-outs. Is it uncertainty in your job, or maybe chaos in your home life? Recognizing these triggers doesn't make you weak; it makes you aware, and awareness is the first step towards change.

### Step 2: Embrace the Unpredictable

The world is a chaotic buffet of unpredictability, and that's not necessarily a bad thing. Begin small: take a different route to work, try a new restaurant without checking the reviews, or let someone else plan your day. Each of these small acts can be monumental in teaching you the art of adaptability.

### Step 3: Delegate Like a Boss

If you're used to micromanaging everything, delegation can feel like you're giving away your limbs. But here's a twist: delegating can lead to more efficiency and even better results. Start with low-risk tasks. Trusting others isn't just about easing your workload; it's about building mutual trust and respect—cornerstones of any successful relationship, whether personal or professional.

### Step 4: Accept Imperfection

Here's a fun fact: Perfection is a myth, much like the Loch Ness Monster. It's talked about a lot but rarely, if ever, seen. Work on accepting that flaws are part of the human experience. This doesn't mean you strive for mediocrity but that you recognize not everything has to be flawless to be valuable.

### Step 5: Reflect and Reassess

Make it a habit to reflect on situations where you let go of control. How did it make you feel? Anxious? Liberated? Probably a bit of both. Reflection helps you understand the benefits of your actions and can reinforce your resolve to continue this practice.

## The Outcome of Letting Go

By now, you might notice a pattern: letting go doesn't result in the apocalypse. In fact, it often leads to better outcomes. Freed from the chains of controlling every detail, you can embrace a fuller, more enriching life experience. You'll likely find that you're more resilient, more open to change, and even happier.

## Final Thoughts

Letting go of control is not about surrendering to chaos but about choosing your battles wisely. It's about realizing that while you can influence your destiny, you can't dictate every aspect of the journey. Life's too short to spend it battling an army of windmills. Instead, aim to flow with the currents of life—sometimes, they'll take you to unexpected and amazing places.

So, the next time you find yourself gripping the wheel of control too tightly, remember this: loosen up a bit, enjoy the ride, and trust that you'll handle the curves and bumps along the way just fine. After all, it's in the unpredictability of life that we truly find joy, growth, and, occasionally, a good laugh at our own expense.

# CHAPTER 7:
## FINDING BEAUTY IN THE JOURNEY

In our pursuit of a picture-perfect life, mapped out with precision and adorned with predictable milestones, we often forget the value and vitality brought forth by unexpected detours. Life, as we live it, rarely follows a neatly drawn line; instead, it meanders, throwing in curves and unexpected twists that not only test our resolve but also enhance our experiences. Embracing these imperfections not only enriches our journey but often leads us to unexpected opportunities.

Imagine you're set on a particular career path, one you've been eyeing since high school. Your plan is laid out: college, internship, then climb the corporate ladder. But what happens when, along the way, you stumble upon a startup opportunity with a friend? It's not part of the plan, but taking that leap could diversify your experience far beyond what any corporate job could offer. Here, the beauty lies not in the deviation itself but in your capacity to adapt and grow, qualities that are invaluable in both personal and professional realms.

Financial education guru Robert Kiyosaki often emphasizes the power of financial literacy, but equally important is 'life literacy', which means understanding that the richest experiences often come from unplanned events. For instance, consider the concept of investment. Conventional wisdom suggests sticking to tried and tested routes—mutual funds, stocks, bonds. However, sometimes the best returns come from unexpected quarters. Maybe it's a small tech firm or a friend's new business venture. The principle remains the same: high risk can lead to high reward. The unpredictability of life, much like the market's fluctuations, isn't something to fear but to embrace as a potential for greater growth. Moreover, life's setbacks and failures are not merely obstacles; they are necessary educators. The loss of a job, as daunting as it may seem, might open more doors than it closes. It pushes you to reconsider your path—perhaps to start your own business or to switch industries. These moments force us out of complacency, challenging us to leverage our skills and passions in ways we hadn't before considered. They're not interruptions in our story; they are essential chapters.

In our personal lives, too, the unexpected moments often lead to the most profound growth. Relationships are a prime example. They are seldom linear. People come and go, sometimes unpredictably so, but each interaction has the potential to teach us something valuable about ourselves and others. Whether it's learning to be more empathetic or understanding different viewpoints, the twists and turns in our relationships shape us significantly.

The richness of life's journey also comes from its ability to surprise and delight in small, everyday moments. Imagine walking the same route every day and one day deciding to turn down a different street. That choice could lead you to a new café, a quaint bookstore, or a park you never knew existed. These small discoveries add layers of joy and wonder to our daily existence, reminding us that there is always something new to be discovered, even in the most familiar environments.

So, how do we navigate this imperfect path with grace? The first step is acceptance. Accept that life is inherently unpredictable, and that's not a flaw—it's a feature. Next is adaptability; being flexible with your plans allows you to make the most of opportunities as they arise, even if they're not what you initially envisioned. And finally, embrace continuous learning. Every unexpected turn is a chance to learn something new, whether it's a skill, a life lesson, or an insight into your own resilience and capability.

In a world where the pace of life is all too often dictated by schedules, deadlines, and incessant digital notifications, it's easy to lose sight of the present moment and the simple blessings it holds. However, the practice of gratitude and mindfulness can transform our everyday experiences, enriching our lives far beyond the material wealth we often chase.

## Gratitude: The Foundation of Abundance

Gratitude isn't just about saying "thank you" or sending out a polite note. It's a profound acknowledgment of the value that something or someone adds to your life. It's recognizing the positive aspects of your life and acknowledging that some of these aspects come from external contributions.

Whether it's appreciating a stable job, a supportive friend, or simply being thankful for a sunny day, gratitude shifts your focus from what your life lacks to the abundance that is already present.

From a financial perspective, gratitude can directly influence how you manage your wealth. When you appreciate what you already have, the incessant need for more can diminish. You become more prudent with your spending, saving, and investing because you are no longer operating from a mindset of scarcity but one of sufficiency. This doesn't mean you halt your financial progress; rather, you pursue it with a mindset that values quality over quantity and long-term satisfaction over short-term gratification.

## Mindfulness: The Art of Presence

Mindfulness, often spoken in the same breath as gratitude, involves maintaining a moment-by-moment awareness of our thoughts, feelings, bodily sensations, and surrounding environment. It's about being fully present in the now, not lost in past regrets or future anxieties. In the context of personal finance, mindfulness could mean conscious spending—being aware of why you're spending what you're spending and how it impacts your financial goals. This might look like pausing before making a purchase to ask yourself whether it's necessary or if it's merely an impulsive buy triggered by stress or excitement.

In daily life, mindfulness can transform mundane activities into moments of joy and discovery. For example, eating is something we often do on autopilot, perhaps while multitasking or watching TV.

Mindful eating involves being fully present with the experience—savoring each bite, acknowledging the flavors, and even considering the origins of the food. This not only enhances the enjoyment of eating but can lead to healthier dietary habits as you become more attuned to your body's needs and signals.

## Practical Steps to a Mindful and Grateful Life

1. **Start with a Gratitude Journal**: Every evening, jot down three things you were grateful for that day. This simple practice can shift your mindset over time, helping you spot the positive more readily than the negative.
2. **Meditate Daily**: Even five minutes of meditation can help increase mindfulness, reduce stress, and enhance overall focus. Apps or guided sessions can help if you're a beginner.
3. **Mindful Mornings**: Spend the first few minutes of your morning sitting quietly, setting a calm tone for the day. Avoid the urge to check your phone the moment you wake up. Instead, use this time to plan your day with intention.
4. **Smart Financial Checks**: Once a week, review your spending and savings plans mindfully. Assess what purchases brought you genuine satisfaction and which ones were unfulfilling. Adjust your future budgets accordingly.

5. **Engage Fully**: Whether it's a conversation or a work task, give it your full attention. This not only improves your effectiveness but also enhances your relationships and work quality.

Incorporating gratitude and mindfulness into our lives isn't just about improving personal well-being; it's about fundamentally transforming how we engage with the world. These practices encourage us to slow down, appreciate what we have, and make more intentional choices. In a society that often equates value with productivity and success with accumulation, choosing to live gratefully and mindfully can be a radical act of personal empowerment.

Living a life rich with gratitude and mindfulness doesn't require monumental changes. It starts with small, daily actions that accumulate to produce profound impacts. By choosing to engage fully in each moment and appreciate the simple joys, we enrich our experiences, deepen our relationships, and navigate the world with a sense of peace and fulfillment that transcends material wealth.

## The Value of Every Step: Learning from Life's Challenges

In life, as in business, it's often our challenges and imperfections that carve the deepest insights into our character and capabilities. Viewing each challenge and imperfection as a valuable lesson and an opportunity for personal growth is more than a mindset; it's a strategic approach to life that fosters resilience, innovation, and, ultimately, success.

## Challenges as Opportunities

Every challenge presents a unique opportunity to learn something new about ourselves, the situation, and the potential solutions. For example, in the business world, a failing product line isn't just a setback—it's a chance to analyze market trends, customer preferences, and internal processes. This analysis can lead to a revamped product that better meets consumer needs or a new service offering that opens additional revenue streams. This concept isn't limited to business. In personal life, a relationship conflict, a setback in health, or an unexpected financial strain are not just problems to be solved. They are opportunities to develop deeper understanding and patience and to fortify our problem-solving skills. Each of these moments is a question posed by life, asking us how much we've learned and how we can apply it moving forward.

## Imperfections as Lessons

Similarly, our imperfections, whether they manifest as skills we haven't mastered or traits we struggle with, are not failings but signposts for growth. A leader who struggles with delegation, for instance, has a clear path for improvement that involves developing trust in their team and honing their management skills. Each attempt at delegation is a mini-experiment in leadership growth, offering insights that gradually shape a more effective leader.

On a personal level, consider someone who struggles with saving money. The imperfection here isn't just in their financial habits but in their relationship with money. Recognizing this can open doors to learning about financial planning and the psychological aspects of spending, leading to more disciplined and informed money management.

## Practical Steps for Learning from Every Step

1. **Embrace Reflection**: After encountering a challenge, take time to reflect. What went wrong? What went right? What could be done differently next time? This reflection turns experience into valuable lessons.
2. **Set Learning Goals**: For each major challenge, set a specific learning goal. If you're facing a tough negotiation, your goal

might be to improve your negotiation techniques. This focus turns the challenge into a learning experience.

3. **Seek Feedback**: Often, our own perceptions of our challenges and imperfections are limited. By seeking feedback from others, we can gain additional insights and alternative perspectives that enhance our learning.

4. **Keep a Growth Journal**: Track your challenges, the actions you took, and the outcomes. Over time, this journal can provide concrete evidence of your growth and remind you of the lessons learned along the way.

5. **Celebrate Small Wins**: Learning from challenges can be daunting. Celebrate small victories along the way to maintain motivation. Each step forward is progress and should be recognized as such.

## Long-Term Benefits of a Learning Mindset

Adopting this approach has profound long-term benefits. Professionally, it makes you more adaptable and innovative, qualities that are invaluable in today's fast-paced business environment. Personally, it enhances your resilience, making you better equipped to handle whatever life throws your way.

Moreover, this mindset can transform your interpersonal relationships. By viewing misunderstandings or conflicts as learning opportunities, you foster a more empathetic and cooperative environment, whether at home or at work. Learning from every step by viewing each challenge and imperfection as a lesson is a powerful approach to life. It cultivates a resilient, proactive, and innovative mindset that not only prepares you to face life's challenges but also to seize its opportunities.

Each step, with its inherent lesson, builds a stronger, more capable individual, poised to achieve greater success and personal fulfillment.

Remember, it's not the challenges that define us but how we choose to learn and grow from them.

## The Practical Guide to Cultivating Daily Gratitude

In a fast-paced world, where ambition often overshadows appreciation, establishing a habit of gratitude can profoundly affect both our mental and financial well-being. Gratitude isn't merely about giving thanks; it's a practical strategy that can enhance decision-making, improve relationships, and even manage financial stress more effectively. Here's how you can cultivate a powerful practice of gratitude with simple daily habits.

## Morning Gratitude Sessions

Begin each day by setting aside a few moments for gratitude. Before the rush of daily responsibilities takes hold, find a quiet space. You don't need a meditation cushion or a yoga mat; sitting on the edge of your bed works just as well. Spend a few minutes thinking about what you're grateful for. It could be as profound as family and friends or as simple as the cup of coffee you look forward to each morning. This practice tunes your mind to a positive frequency, positively influencing how you perceive challenges and interact with others throughout the day.

## Grateful Journaling

While morning gratitude sessions set the tone for the day, maintaining a gratitude journal can help sustain that perspective. Each evening, jot down three things that you were grateful for that day.

These don't need to be groundbreaking events. Often, it's the small things that leave the most significant impact—perhaps a productive work meeting, a stranger's smile, or a delicious lunch. This habit not only ends your day on a positive note but also serves as a tangible record of all the good in your life, which can be incredibly uplifting during tougher times.

## Mindful Meals

Turn meals into an opportunity for gratitude. Before you begin eating, take a moment to appreciate the food on your plate. Consider the chain of events that brought the meal to your table—the farmers, the transporters, the grocers, and perhaps a family member who prepared it.

This practice not only fosters gratitude but also deepens your connection to the world around you, enhancing mindfulness and reducing the likelihood of mindless eating, which is often driven by stress rather than hunger.

## Appreciation in Action

Gratitude becomes more potent when it is expressed. Make it a point to express your appreciation to others daily. Whether it's complimenting a colleague on a well-done presentation, thanking your partner for their support, or acknowledging a friend's good advice, expressing gratitude strengthens relationships and builds a supportive network—elements that are crucial for both personal satisfaction and professional success.

## Tech-Assisted Gratitude

Leverage technology to remind you to stay grateful. Set daily reminders on your phone or computer to pause and reflect on something you're grateful for. There are also apps designed to prompt and record expressions of gratitude. This blend of traditional practice and modern technology makes maintaining a gratitude habit both easy and accessible, especially for those with a busy lifestyle.

## Random Acts of Kindness

Once a week, commit to performing a random act of kindness. It could be paying for the next person's coffee, donating to a charity, or helping a neighbor with chores. Acts of kindness and generosity ignite feelings of gratitude, not just for the recipient but for the giver as well. This reciprocal appreciation is powerful, promoting a sense of community and interconnectedness.

## Reflection on Challenges

At the end of each week, reflect on the challenges you faced. Identify what they taught you and try to find aspects for which you are grateful. Perhaps a difficult project improved your skills, or a misunderstanding with a friend deepened your communication. Viewing challenges through the lens of gratitude reduces stress and cultivates a resilient and positive mindset. Incorporating these simple practices into your daily routine can transform gratitude from a fleeting feeling to a foundational habit. The benefits extend beyond personal happiness, influencing your financial decisions, business relationships, and overall approach to life. By nurturing gratitude, you're not just enriching your own life; you're enhancing the lives of those around you, creating a ripple effect of positivity and prosperity. Remember, gratitude is not just about recognizing good after it happens; it's about continuously acknowledging and appreciating the good as it unfolds.

# CHAPTER 8:
## THE PRACTICE OF SELF-CARE

In the world of wealth creation, the focus is often on financial strategies, investment opportunities, and business acumen. However, there's a critical component that often gets overlooked: self-care. As someone who has spent years teaching people how to attain financial independence, I can tell you this—your mental, emotional, and physical health are the foundation upon which all your success is built. Without them, everything else crumbles.

## The Mental Edge

Imagine you're a race car driver. Your mind is the engine. If it's not maintained properly, no matter how skilled a driver you are, you're not going to win the race. Self-care, in this context, means giving your mind the attention it needs to function at its best.

1. **Prioritize Rest:** One of the simplest yet most powerful forms of self-care is adequate sleep. Your brain needs time to recharge. Without proper rest, your cognitive functions diminish, decision-making falters, and creativity dwindles. Prioritize sleep as if your business depends on it—because it does.

2. **Stay Informed, Not Overwhelmed:** Information is critical, but in today's world, it's easy to become overwhelmed. Curate your sources of information. Focus on what helps you grow and filter out the noise. This keeps your mind sharp and focused on what truly matters.

3. **Mental Exercises:** Just like physical exercise keeps your body in shape, mental exercises keep your brain agile. Engage in activities that challenge your thinking—puzzles, strategy games, learning new skills. This not only improves your mental acuity but also prepares you to tackle complex business problems.

# Emotional Resilience

Emotional health is about resilience—being able to bounce back from setbacks, handle stress, and maintain a positive outlook. It's not just about feeling good; it's about being able to perform under pressure.

1. **Practice Mindfulness:** Mindfulness is about being present in the moment. It helps reduce stress and increase emotional control. Simple practices like meditation, deep breathing, or even just taking a walk can make a significant difference in your emotional well-being.

2. **Build a Support Network:** No one succeeds alone. Surround yourself with people who support you emotionally. This could be family, friends, or a mentor. Having a support network provides a safety net, offering encouragement and perspective when times get tough.

3. **Express Gratitude:** It might sound clichéd, but gratitude has a profound impact on your emotional health. Regularly take time to reflect on what you're thankful for. This shifts your focus from what's going wrong to what's going right, fostering a more positive outlook.

# Physical Vitality

Your body is your vessel. If it's not well-maintained, your capacity to achieve and enjoy success diminishes. Physical health directly impacts your energy levels, productivity, and overall well-being.

1. **Regular Exercise:** Incorporate physical activity into your daily routine. This doesn't mean you need to become a gym rat. Find activities you enjoy—whether it's walking, cycling, or playing a sport. Regular exercise boosts your energy, improves your mood, and enhances your productivity.

2. **Nutrition Matters:** You wouldn't put the wrong fuel in a high-performance car, so why do it to your body? Eat a balanced diet rich in nutrients. Avoid processed foods and excessive sugar. Proper nutrition fuels your body and mind, giving you the energy and clarity needed to tackle your goals.

3. **Routine Health Checks:** Regular health check-ups are a form of proactive self-care. Identify potential health issues early and take steps to address them. This approach ensures you stay in peak physical condition, ready to face whatever challenges come your way.

## Integrating Self-Care into Your Life

Self-care isn't a one-time event; it's a continuous process. It should be integrated into your daily routine. Here are some practical tips to help you embed self-care into your busy life.

1. **Schedule It:** Just like you would schedule a meeting or a deadline, schedule time for self-care. Whether it's a workout, a meditation session, or just a quiet moment to yourself, put it on your calendar and treat it as non-negotiable.

2. **Set Boundaries:** Learn to say no. Protect your time and energy. This means setting boundaries with work, with people, and even with yourself. Respecting these boundaries ensures you have the space to take care of yourself.

3. **Reflect and Adjust:** Regularly take time to reflect on your self-care practices. What's working? What's not? Be willing to

adjust your routines to better serve your mental, emotional, and physical health.

When you prioritize self-care, the benefits extend beyond just your personal well-being. You become more effective in your work, a better leader, and a more engaged individual. This ripple effect can transform not just your life but the lives of those around you.

1. **Enhanced Productivity:** A well-rested, well-nourished, and mentally sharp person is far more productive. You make better decisions, work more efficiently, and are more creative. This directly impacts your bottom line.

2. **Positive Relationships:** When you take care of your emotional health, you are better equipped to handle relationships—both personal and professional. You communicate more effectively, handle conflicts better, and create a more positive environment.

3. **Inspiring Others:** By prioritizing self-care, you set an example for others. Whether it's your family, your team, or your community, your actions can inspire others to take better care of themselves. This creates a culture of health and well-being that benefits everyone.

In the pursuit of financial success, don't neglect the most important asset you have: yourself. Self-care is not a luxury; it's a necessity. It's the foundation that supports all your endeavors. By prioritizing your mental, emotional, and physical health, you equip yourself with the tools to achieve and sustain success. Remember, wealth is not just about money; it's about having the freedom and well-being to enjoy the fruits of your labor. Invest in yourself—it's the best investment you can make.

Taking care of yourself holistically is a game-changer. It's like investing in the most valuable asset you have—yourself. When you care for your mental, physical, and spiritual dimensions, you create a balanced life that can withstand the ups and downs. This approach isn't just about feeling good; it's about building resilience and achieving long-term success. Let's break it down in a straightforward, no-nonsense way.

First, let's talk about the mental aspect. Your mind is your powerhouse. If it's cluttered with negativity or stress, it's hard to function effectively. Think of it like running a business with outdated equipment. You wouldn't do that, right? So, why let your mind operate on outdated, harmful thoughts? Start by practicing mindfulness. It's not some mystical practice; it's about being present and aware. For example, take five minutes each day to sit quietly and focus on your breathing. This simple act can reduce stress and improve clarity. It's like rebooting your computer—clearing out the junk and starting fresh.

Reading is another crucial part of mental care. Books are like mentors who guide you through their pages. They offer new perspectives and ideas that can spark innovation in your life. Take Warren Buffett, for example. He spends hours each day reading, believing it's key to his success. If it works for him, it can work for you too. Pick up a book that interests you, whether it's on personal development, a novel, or even a biography. The goal is to keep your mind active and engaged.

Physical health is equally important. You wouldn't ignore maintenance on a valuable piece of machinery, so don't neglect your body. Exercise regularly, but don't think you need to become a gym rat. Find something you enjoy, whether it's walking, swimming, or yoga. The key is consistency. Consider someone like Richard Branson, who swears by his daily exercise routine. It keeps him energized and ready to tackle any challenge.

Diet plays a critical role, too. What you fuel your body with affects your performance. Eating a balanced diet rich in vegetables, fruits, lean proteins, and whole grains can enhance your energy levels and overall health. Avoid the trap of fast food and sugary snacks. They may be convenient, but they drag you down in the long run. Think of your body as a high-performance car. Would you put low-grade fuel in it? Of course not. Treat your body with the same respect. Then there's the spiritual dimension. This isn't about religion necessarily; it's about finding purpose and meaning in your life. It's the foundation that supports everything else. When you have a clear sense of purpose, you're more motivated and driven. Oprah Winfrey often speaks about the importance of aligning your work with your purpose. She believes that when you do what you love, success follows naturally.

Meditation can be a powerful tool for spiritual care. It helps you connect with your inner self and understand what truly matters to you. Take a few minutes each day to meditate, reflecting on your goals and values. It doesn't require any special skills, just a bit of time and patience. Over time, you'll find that it brings a sense of peace and direction to your life.

Connecting with others is also part of spiritual health. Humans are social creatures, and we thrive on relationships. Surround yourself with positive, supportive people who uplift you. Build a network of friends, family, and mentors who can offer guidance and support. Remember the saying, "You are the average of the five people you spend the most time with." Choose those people wisely.

Lastly, consider giving back to the community. Volunteering or helping others in need can provide a profound sense of fulfillment. It's about contributing to something bigger than yourself. Look at Bill Gates, who, after achieving monumental success, turned his focus to philanthropy. His foundation has made a significant impact on global health and education, showing that true wealth lies in what you give back. Incorporating a holistic approach to your well-being isn't just a one-time effort; it's a continuous process. It's about making small, consistent changes that add up over time. Start with one area, make improvements, and then move on to the next. It's like building a strong, diverse portfolio. Each aspect—mental, physical, and spiritual—adds value and stability to your life.

Think of it this way: you wouldn't invest all your money in a single stock. Diversification is key to minimizing risk and maximizing returns. The same goes for your well-being. By nurturing each aspect of your being, you create a balanced, resilient life. It's not about perfection but progress. Each step you take towards a more holistic approach is an investment in your future.

So, take action today. Start small, but think big. Invest in your mind by reading and practicing mindfulness. Care for your body with regular exercise and a healthy diet. Nurture your spirit by finding your purpose, meditating, and connecting with others. It's a comprehensive strategy that, like any good investment, requires time and patience but promises significant returns. Your life, after all, is your most valuable asset. Treat it with the care it deserves.

Creating a self-care routine that truly resonates with your individual needs and preferences is like designing a custom-made suit. It's tailored specifically for you, ensuring that each element fits perfectly into your lifestyle and addresses your unique requirements. Here's a straightforward guide to help you design a self-care routine that works for you.

**Step 1: Assess Your Needs**

Start by taking an honest inventory of your life. Ask yourself:

- What areas of my life feel most stressed or neglected?
- Where do I feel most fulfilled and balanced?
- What activities bring me joy and relaxation?

By answering these questions, you'll identify the key areas that need attention. Maybe you're mentally exhausted, physically drained, or spiritually disconnected. Understanding your starting point is crucial.

**Step 2: Set Clear Goals**

Once you've assessed your needs, set specific, realistic goals. These goals should address the areas you identified in your self-assessment. For example:

- Improve mental health by reducing stress.
- Enhance physical fitness and energy levels.
- Connect more deeply with your spiritual self.

Make sure your goals are achievable and measurable. Instead of saying, "I want to be less stressed," try, "I will practice mindfulness for 10 minutes every day."

**Step 3: Choose Activities That Align With Your Goals**

Now, select activities that support your goals. Here are some examples:

**For Mental Health:**

- Mindfulness or meditation practices.
- Journaling to process thoughts and emotions.
- Reading books or articles that inspire and educate.

**For Physical Health:**

- Regular exercise, such as walking, yoga, or weight training.
- Eating a balanced diet with plenty of fruits, vegetables, lean proteins, and whole grains.
- Ensuring adequate sleep by maintaining a consistent bedtime routine.

**For Spiritual Health:**

- Meditation or prayer.
- Spending time in nature.
- Engaging in activities that align with your values and passions.

Choose activities that you enjoy and can realistically integrate into your daily life.

## Step 4: Create a Schedule

Consistency is key to a successful self-care routine. Create a schedule that incorporates your chosen activities. Start small to ensure you don't feel overwhelmed. Here's an example of a simple daily routine:

- **Morning**: 10 minutes of mindfulness meditation and a healthy breakfast.
- **Lunchtime**: A brisk 20-minute walk.
- **Evening**: Reading a book for 30 minutes before bed, practicing gratitude by listing three things you're thankful for.

Adjust the schedule to fit your lifestyle. If mornings are hectic, shift some activities to the evening.

## Step 5: Monitor and Adjust

After implementing your routine, monitor how it's working for you. Pay attention to how you feel physically, mentally, and spiritually. Are you meeting your goals? Are there any activities that feel more like a chore than a pleasure?

Be flexible and willing to adjust your routine. Maybe you find that a different type of exercise is more enjoyable, or a new meditation app makes your practice more effective. Regularly reassess and tweak your routine to keep it fresh and aligned with your needs.

### Step 6: Incorporate Variety and Fun

Self-care shouldn't feel like another task on your to-do list. Incorporate variety and fun into your routine to keep it engaging. Try new activities, like a dance class, a cooking workshop, or a weekend hike. The key is to keep exploring and enjoying the process.

### Step 7: Build a Support System

Having a support system can significantly enhance your self-care efforts. Share your goals with friends or family members who can offer encouragement and accountability. Consider joining a group or community that shares similar interests, whether it's a book club, a fitness class, or a meditation group.

### Step 8: Practice Self-Compassion

Remember, self-care is about nurturing yourself, not about perfection. Be kind to yourself if you miss a day or don't stick to your routine perfectly. Life happens, and flexibility is essential. What matters is your overall commitment to taking care of yourself.

### Step 9: Celebrate Your Progress

Acknowledge and celebrate your progress, no matter how small. Reflect on the positive changes you've noticed in your life since starting your self-care routine. This can reinforce your commitment and motivate you to continue.

### Step 10: Keep Evolving

As you grow and change, so will your self-care needs. Periodically revisit your routine and goals. Stay open to new practices and activities that might better serve you as time goes on. Self-care is a lifelong journey, not a destination.

Creating a personalized self-care routine is a powerful step towards a balanced and fulfilling life. By taking the time to assess your needs, set clear goals, and choose activities that resonate with you, you invest in your well-being. Remember, the best self-care routine is one that feels right for you and fits seamlessly into your life. Start small, stay consistent, and enjoy the journey of caring for yourself.

# CHAPTER 9:
## CULTIVATING RESILIENCE

Resilience is the cornerstone of navigating life's inevitable ups and downs. At its core, resilience is the process of building inner strength to effectively cope with life's challenges. This inner strength isn't something people are born with; it's developed over time through experiences, practices, and conscious effort. Let's delve into what forms the foundation of resilience and how you can cultivate it.

## Understanding Resilience

Resilience is not about avoiding stress or adversity; it's about learning how to face these challenges head-on and emerge stronger. It's like a muscle that gets stronger with use. The more you exercise your resilience, the better you become at handling life's difficulties.

## Building Inner Strength

1. **Self-Awareness:** The first step in building resilience is becoming self-aware. Understand your strengths and weaknesses, your triggers, and your coping mechanisms. Self-awareness involves regularly reflecting on your thoughts, emotions, and behaviors. It helps you recognize when you are stressed or overwhelmed and allows you to take proactive steps to manage your response.

2. **Emotional Regulation:** Being able to manage your emotions is crucial. This doesn't mean suppressing them; it means understanding and expressing them in healthy ways. Techniques such as mindfulness, meditation, and deep

breathing exercises can help you stay calm and focused in stressful situations. When you can regulate your emotions, you can think more clearly and make better decisions.

3. **Optimism:** Maintaining a positive outlook doesn't mean ignoring problems; it means seeing challenges as opportunities for growth. Optimism helps you stay motivated and focused on solutions rather than problems. This mindset encourages perseverance, which is essential for overcoming obstacles.

4. **Flexibility:** Life is unpredictable, and resilience involves being adaptable. Flexibility means being open to change and willing to adjust your plans when necessary. It also involves being able to view setbacks as temporary and not as defining moments. This adaptability allows you to bounce back more quickly from adversity.

5. **Problem-Solving Skills:** Effective problem-solving is a key component of resilience. When faced with a challenge, break it down into manageable parts, brainstorm possible solutions, and take decisive action. This systematic approach can prevent feelings of being overwhelmed and help you tackle issues more efficiently.

## Practical Strategies for Cultivating Resilience

1. **Build Strong Relationships:** Having a supportive network is invaluable. Friends, family, and colleagues can provide emotional support, practical advice, and different perspectives. Don't hesitate to lean on your support system when needed, and be there for others in return.

2. **Set Realistic Goals:** Set achievable goals and work steadily towards them. This sense of purpose and direction can keep you focused during tough times. Celebrate small victories along the way to maintain motivation.

3. **Take Care of Your Physical Health:** Physical well-being is closely linked to mental health. Regular exercise, a balanced diet, and adequate sleep can enhance your mood, energy levels, and overall resilience. When your body is strong, your mind is better equipped to handle stress.

4. **Practice Mindfulness and Meditation:** These practices can help you stay present and reduce anxiety about the future. Mindfulness involves paying attention to the present moment without judgment, which can help you manage stress and stay grounded.

5. **Develop a Growth Mindset:** Embrace challenges as opportunities to learn and grow. A growth mindset, as proposed by psychologist Carol Dweck, is the belief that abilities and intelligence can be developed through effort and learning. This perspective fosters resilience by encouraging continuous improvement and learning from setbacks.

6. **Self-Compassion:** Be kind to yourself, especially in times of failure or disappointment. Self-compassion involves treating yourself with the same understanding and kindness that you would offer to a friend. It helps you maintain a positive self-view and recover more quickly from setbacks.

## The Role of Experience

Experience plays a vital role in building resilience. Each challenge you face and overcome strengthens your inner resolve and teaches valuable lessons. Over time, these experiences build a repository of coping strategies and confidence, reinforcing your ability to handle future adversities. Reflecting on past challenges and recognizing your growth can boost your resilience further.

Resilience is the process of building inner strength to effectively cope with life's challenges. It involves a combination of self-awareness, emotional regulation, optimism, flexibility, and problem-solving skills. By practicing these elements and adopting practical strategies such as building strong relationships, setting realistic goals, taking care of your physical health, and embracing a growth mindset, you can cultivate a resilient mindset. Remember, resilience is not a fixed trait but a dynamic process that evolves with each experience and challenge you face. Through conscious effort and practice, you can develop the inner strength to navigate life's adversities and thrive despite them.

Harnessing inner strength to foster resilience and the ability to persevere through adversity is essential for personal growth and success. This process involves developing strategies that help you maintain stability and strength, even in the face of challenges. Here's how you can cultivate resilience and build your capacity to persevere:

## 1. Cultivate a Positive Mindset

A positive mindset is the bedrock of resilience. It involves viewing challenges as opportunities rather than obstacles.

- **Practice Gratitude:** Regularly acknowledge what you are thankful for. This practice can shift your focus from what's wrong to what's right, fostering a more positive outlook.
- **Affirmations:** Use positive affirmations to reinforce your belief in your capabilities. Statements like "I am capable of overcoming this" can help you stay motivated.
- **Visualize Success:** Spend time visualizing your success. Imagine overcoming obstacles and achieving your goals. This mental practice can build confidence and reduce anxiety.

## 2. Develop Strong Relationships

Having a supportive network is crucial for resilience. Strong relationships provide emotional support and practical advice.

- **Build Connections:** Invest time in building and nurturing relationships with family, friends, and colleagues. These connections can offer support and perspective during tough times.
- **Seek Support:** Don't hesitate to reach out for help when needed. Sharing your struggles with trusted individuals can provide relief and insight.
- **Join Communities:** Engage in groups or communities that share your interests. These communities can offer a sense of belonging and additional support.

## 3. Enhance Emotional Regulation

Managing your emotions effectively is vital for resilience. Emotional regulation helps you stay calm and focused during adversity.

- **Mindfulness and Meditation:** Practice mindfulness and meditation to stay present and manage stress. These practices can help you observe your thoughts and emotions without getting overwhelmed.
- **Breathing Techniques:** Use deep breathing exercises to calm your mind and body. Techniques like diaphragmatic breathing can reduce stress and improve focus.
- **Express Emotions:** Find healthy ways to express your emotions, such as journaling, talking to a friend, or engaging in creative activities like painting or music.

## 4. Adopt a Growth Mindset

A growth mindset, as proposed by Carol Dweck, involves believing that abilities and intelligence can be developed through effort and learning.

- **Embrace Challenges:** View challenges as opportunities to learn and grow. This perspective encourages persistence and innovation.
- **Learn from Failures:** Instead of viewing failures as setbacks, see them as learning experiences. Analyze what went wrong and how you can improve.
- **Celebrate Effort:** Focus on the effort you put into tasks rather than just the outcomes. Recognizing your hard work can boost motivation and resilience.

## 5. Set Realistic Goals

Setting and achieving realistic goals can build confidence and resilience.

- **Break Down Goals:** Divide larger goals into smaller, manageable steps. This approach makes tasks less daunting and more achievable.
- **Prioritize Tasks:** Identify the most important tasks and focus on them first. Prioritizing can help you manage time and resources effectively.
- **Track Progress:** Regularly review your progress towards your goals. Celebrate small victories to maintain motivation and momentum.

## 6. Maintain Physical Health

Physical health significantly impacts mental and emotional resilience.

- **Regular Exercise:** Engage in regular physical activity. Exercise releases endorphins, which can improve mood and reduce stress.
- **Healthy Diet:** Eat a balanced diet rich in fruits, vegetables, lean proteins, and whole grains. Proper nutrition supports overall well-being and energy levels.

- **Adequate Sleep:** Ensure you get enough sleep each night. Quality sleep is essential for cognitive function and emotional stability.

## 7. Foster Self-Compassion

Being kind to yourself, especially during difficult times, is essential for resilience.

- **Practice Self-Kindness:** Treat yourself with the same kindness and understanding you would offer a friend. Acknowledge your efforts and achievements, even if they seem small.
- **Mindful Self-Awareness:** Be aware of your self-talk and challenge negative thoughts. Replace them with more compassionate and realistic perspectives.
- **Forgive Yourself:** Understand that everyone makes mistakes. Forgive yourself for past mistakes and focus on what you can do differently moving forward.

## 8. Build Problem-Solving Skills

Effective problem-solving skills can enhance resilience by providing practical ways to handle challenges.

- **Identify Problems Clearly:** Clearly define the problem you are facing. Understanding the issue thoroughly is the first step towards solving it.
- **Brainstorm Solutions:** Generate multiple possible solutions. Consider the pros and cons of each option before deciding on the best course of action.
- **Take Action:** Implement the chosen solution and monitor its effectiveness. Be prepared to adjust your approach if necessary.

## 9. Maintain Flexibility

Flexibility allows you to adapt to changing circumstances and stay resilient.

- **Be Open to Change:** Embrace change as a natural part of life. Being adaptable can help you handle unexpected challenges more effectively.
- **Stay Curious:** Maintain a curious attitude and be willing to learn new skills or approaches. Continuous learning keeps you adaptable and prepared for future challenges.
- **Reevaluate Goals:** Regularly review and adjust your goals and plans based on current circumstances. Flexibility in your approach can help you stay on track despite obstacles.

Harnessing inner strength to foster resilience and the ability to persevere through adversity involves cultivating a positive mindset, developing strong relationships, enhancing emotional regulation, adopting a growth mindset, setting realistic goals, maintaining physical health, fostering self-compassion, building problem-solving skills, and maintaining flexibility. By integrating these strategies into your daily life, you can build a robust foundation of resilience, enabling you to navigate life's challenges with greater ease and confidence. Remember, resilience is a skill that can be developed and strengthened over time, empowering you to persevere and thrive in the face of adversity.

Resilience is the ability to bounce back from setbacks and adapt to challenging circumstances. It's about how you respond to adversity, not avoiding it. Imagine life as a boxing match. You're going to take hits, but resilience is what keeps you getting back up, round after round, ready to fight again. It's the grit that separates those who merely survive from those who thrive.

Consider the story of J.K. Rowling. Before she became a literary sensation with her Harry Potter series, she faced numerous rejections. She was a single mother living on welfare, struggling to make ends meet. But she had a vision and a resilience that kept her moving forward. Each rejection letter she received was just another step on the ladder to success. She didn't see them as failures but as feedback. This resilience is what eventually led her to become one of the most successful authors of our time. Resilience isn't just about enduring hardship; it's about finding a way to thrive in spite of it. Take Elon Musk, for example. He faced multiple setbacks with SpaceX, including several failed rocket launches. Yet, each failure was a lesson learned. He didn't see failure as the end but as a crucial part of the journey. Musk's resilience allowed him to push through these setbacks and eventually succeed in revolutionizing space travel. So, how do you develop this kind of resilience? One key strategy is maintaining a positive outlook. This isn't about blind optimism but about realistic positivity. When faced with a challenge, focus on what you can control and let go of what you can't. This mindset helps you to stay motivated and engaged, even when things are tough.

Another example is Oprah Winfrey. She faced numerous challenges early in life, including poverty and abuse. But she didn't let these circumstances define her. Instead, she used her experiences as fuel to drive her success. She focused on what she could control—her education, her career choices, and her personal growth. This focus helped her to become one of the most influential media moguls in the world.

Developing resilience also involves setting realistic goals. Break down your larger goals into manageable steps. This makes it easier to see progress and maintain motivation. Think of it like running a marathon. You don't focus on the entire 26 miles at once. You focus on each step, each mile, and before you know it, you've crossed the finish line.

Steve Jobs is another prime example. When he was ousted from Apple, the company he co-founded, it could have been a devastating blow. Instead, Jobs used this setback as an opportunity. He started new ventures, like Pixar, and eventually returned to Apple, leading it to unprecedented success. He didn't let a major professional setback derail his vision. Instead, he adapted, learned, and came back stronger. Building a support network is another crucial component of resilience. Surround yourself with people who believe in you and who can offer advice and encouragement when times are tough. Look at the story of Thomas Edison. When working on the light bulb, he faced countless failures. But he had a team that believed in his vision and supported him through the tough times. This support network was instrumental in his eventual success.

Resilience also means being flexible and open to change. The world is constantly evolving, and those who can adapt will thrive. During the COVID-19 pandemic, many businesses faced unprecedented challenges. Some crumbled under the pressure, while others adapted and found new ways to serve their customers. Restaurants that quickly pivoted to takeout and delivery services, gyms that offered virtual classes, and companies that embraced remote work not only survived but found new opportunities for growth.

Jeff Bezos, the founder of Amazon, embodies this adaptability. Amazon started as an online bookstore, but Bezos had a vision for something much larger. Over the years, he has continuously adapted the business model, exploring new markets and technologies. This willingness to change and adapt is a core component of Amazon's success and a testament to Bezos's resilience.

Another critical aspect of resilience is learning from your mistakes. Failure is an inevitable part of any journey, but it's what you do after you fail that counts. When Michael Jordan was cut from his high school basketball team, he didn't give up. He used it as motivation to work harder and become better. He learned from his mistakes, improved his skills, and eventually became one of the greatest basketball players of all time. Resilience can also be about knowing when to take a break. Pushing through nonstop can lead to burnout. It's important to recognize when you need to step back, rest, and recharge. This isn't a sign of weakness but a strategy for long-term success. Look at athletes—they train hard, but they also know the importance of rest and recovery. It's during these periods that the body heals and grows stronger, preparing them for the next challenge.

Finally, practicing gratitude can enhance resilience. By focusing on what you're thankful for, you can shift your perspective and find strength even in difficult times. During challenging moments, take time to reflect on what's going well. This doesn't negate the difficulty of your situation but can provide a mental boost and remind you of the positive aspects of your life.

Resilience is about bouncing back from setbacks and continuing to move forward. It's about maintaining a positive outlook, setting realistic goals, building a support network, being flexible, learning from mistakes, knowing when to rest, and practicing gratitude. These strategies can help you navigate life's challenges and come out stronger on the other side. Like the greats before us, we all have the capacity for resilience. It's not a trait you're born with but a skill you can develop and strengthen over time.

# CHAPTER 10:
## LIVING AUTHENTICALLY

In a world full of noise and distractions, finding and living by your authentic self is a challenge. Yet, it is one of the most fulfilling endeavors one can undertake.

Authenticity is not just a buzzword or a trending topic; it's the profound alignment of one's actions and life with one's true self and core values. When you live authentically, you don't just exist—you thrive.

## Understanding Authenticity

Authenticity is about being true to who you are, not who others expect you to be. It's about knowing your core values and living in accordance with them.

This concept might sound simple, but it requires deep introspection and courage. The journey to authenticity begins with understanding yourself—your strengths, weaknesses, passions, and fears. It's about peeling back the layers of societal expectations and discovering the real you underneath.

## The Importance of Self-Awareness

Self-awareness is the cornerstone of authenticity. It involves being honest with yourself about what you want from life, what you believe in, and what makes you happy. This honesty can be uncomfortable because it might reveal that you are not living in alignment with your true self. However, this discomfort is necessary for growth. To become self-aware, start by reflecting on your life. What activities make you lose track of time? What values are non-negotiable for you? Who are the people that make you feel energized and alive? Answering these questions can help you identify your true self and core values.

## Aligning Actions with Values

Once you have a clear understanding of your true self and core values, the next step is to align your actions with them. This alignment is where many people struggle. It's easy to get caught up in the expectations of others and the demands of daily life. However, living authentically requires conscious effort and sometimes difficult choices.

For example, if one of your core values is honesty, you need to ensure that your actions reflect this value. This might mean having tough conversations or making decisions that are not popular but are right for you. The key is to consistently evaluate your actions and ensure they are in harmony with your values.

## Overcoming Fear and Societal Pressure

One of the biggest obstacles to living authentically is fear—fear of rejection, fear of failure, fear of standing out. Society often pressures us to conform, to fit in, and to follow a path that is considered "normal." But authenticity requires you to break free from these pressures and embrace your uniqueness. Overcoming fear involves building resilience and developing a mindset that values growth over comfort. It's about understanding that failure is a part of the journey and that rejection often means you are on the right path. Surround yourself with people who support your authentic self and who encourage you to stay true to your values.

## The Benefits of Living Authentically

Living authentically has numerous benefits. It leads to greater fulfillment and happiness because you are living in alignment with your true self. It also fosters deeper and more meaningful relationships because people are drawn to those who are genuine and real. Additionally, authenticity can lead to greater success because you are more likely to pursue opportunities that resonate with your core values and passions.

## Practical Steps to Embrace Authenticity

1. **Reflect Regularly**: Take time to reflect on your actions and whether they align with your core values. Journaling can be a powerful tool for this reflection.
2. **Set Boundaries**: Learn to say no to things that don't align with your values. This might involve setting boundaries with people who pressure you to conform.
3. **Seek Support**: Find a community or a mentor who encourages you to be your authentic self. Surrounding yourself with like-minded individuals can provide the support you need to stay true to yourself.
4. **Take Small Steps**: Start with small actions that align with your values. Over time, these small steps can lead to significant changes in your life.
5. **Embrace Imperfection**: Understand that living authentically doesn't mean being perfect. It's about being real, and sometimes that means making mistakes and learning from them.

In a fast-paced world that constantly tries to mold us into something we are not, staying true to oneself is a revolutionary act. Authenticity is the alignment of your life and actions with your true self and core values. It requires self-awareness, courage, and the willingness to face societal pressures head-on. The journey is not always easy, but the rewards—greater fulfillment, deeper relationships, and true success—are worth it.

Living authentically is about more than just being real; it's about being the best version of yourself. It's about knowing your values, aligning your actions with those values, and embracing your uniqueness. As you embark on this journey, remember that authenticity is a continuous process of growth and self-discovery.

## Celebrating Uniqueness: Embrace Your Authentic Self

In the world of finance and personal growth, there is one principle that stands head and shoulders above the rest: the power of uniqueness. Each individual carries a distinct set of skills, perspectives, and experiences that set them apart from everyone else. This uniqueness is not just an asset; it's a cornerstone of success.

## Understanding the Value of Uniqueness

Uniqueness is often underestimated. In a society that constantly pushes for conformity, we are frequently taught to suppress our individuality. We learn to follow the crowd, adhere to norms, and fit into predefined molds. However, the truth is that your distinctiveness is your greatest strength. It is what makes you, you. It's what you bring to the table that no one else can. Consider the world of business. Every successful entrepreneur, from Steve Jobs to Elon Musk, has achieved greatness not by following the status quo but by embracing their unique vision and perspective. They dared to be different, and in doing so, they created products and services that changed the world. The lesson here is clear: your uniqueness is your competitive edge.

# Embracing Authenticity

Authenticity goes hand in hand with uniqueness. To be authentic means to be true to yourself and to embrace your values, beliefs, and personality without compromise. Authenticity is a magnet that attracts genuine relationships, whether in business or personal life. When you are authentic, you build trust, and trust is the foundation of any successful endeavor.

Authenticity also fosters resilience. When you are true to yourself, you are better equipped to handle challenges and setbacks. You have a clear sense of purpose and direction, which guides you through tough times. You are not easily swayed by external pressures or opinions because you know who you are and what you stand for.

# Leveraging Your Unique Skills and Talents

Every individual possesses a unique set of skills and talents. These are your tools for success. Identifying and leveraging these skills is crucial in carving out your niche. For instance, if you have a knack for numbers, you might excel in finance. If you have a creative mind, the arts or innovation might be your calling.

The key is to recognize your strengths and use them to your advantage. This does not mean that you should ignore your weaknesses, but rather, focus on what you do best. Surround yourself with people who complement your skills and can help you address areas where you are less strong.

# Uniqueness in the Marketplace

In the marketplace, standing out is more important than ever. Consumers are bombarded with choices, and businesses that fail to differentiate themselves often get lost in the noise. Your uniqueness is your brand. It is what makes you memorable and sets you apart from competitors.

Think of companies like Apple or Tesla. They have created strong brands by emphasizing their unique qualities—innovation, design, and a commitment to pushing boundaries. They do not try to be like everyone else; instead, they double down on what makes them different.

## The Courage to Be Different

Embracing your uniqueness requires courage. It means stepping out of your comfort zone and potentially facing criticism or rejection. However, the rewards far outweigh the risks. When you dare to be different, you open up a world of possibilities. You pave the way for innovation and progress, both personally and professionally. It is also important to note that being different does not mean being isolated. Surround yourself with like-minded individuals who value and respect your uniqueness. Build a network of support that encourages you to be your authentic self.

## Practical Steps to Embrace Your Uniqueness

1. **Self-Reflection**: Take time to reflect on your values, beliefs, and strengths. Understand what makes you unique and how you can leverage these qualities in your personal and professional life.
2. **Set Authentic Goals**: Align your goals with your true self. Pursue what genuinely interests and excites you rather than what you think is expected of you.
3. **Embrace Failure**: Understand that failure is a part of the journey. It is through failure that we learn and grow. Do not let the fear of failure prevent you from embracing your uniqueness.

4. **Continuous Learning**: Keep learning and evolving. The world is constantly changing, and staying true to yourself requires adapting to new circumstances while maintaining your core values.
5. **Build a Support Network**: Surround yourself with people who support and encourage your uniqueness. These individuals will help you stay grounded and provide valuable feedback.

Celebrating your uniqueness and embracing authenticity are fundamental to achieving success and fulfillment. Your distinctiveness is your greatest asset, setting you apart in a crowded world. By understanding the value of your unique qualities, leveraging your skills, and having the courage to be different, you can build a life and career that is not only successful but also deeply satisfying.

**Guidelines for Authentic Living: Embracing Your True Self**

Living authentically is a journey of self-discovery and courage. It means living in harmony with your beliefs and confidently expressing your true identity. Here, we will explore practical ways to achieve this, inspired by the straightforward and practical wisdom of Robert T. Kiyosaki.

## Understanding Authenticity

Authenticity is about being true to who you are. It means aligning your actions, decisions, and life with your core values and beliefs. It requires honesty, courage, and a willingness to be vulnerable. The journey to authenticity involves knowing yourself, embracing your uniqueness, and living according to your principles.

## Know Yourself

The first step to living authentically is self-awareness. You need to understand your values, beliefs, strengths, and weaknesses. Self-awareness involves introspection and reflection. Here are some practical steps to enhance self-awareness:

- **Reflection:** Take time daily to reflect on your thoughts and actions. Journaling can be a powerful tool for this.
- **Feedback:** Seek feedback from trusted friends and mentors. They can provide valuable insights into your behavior and how others perceive you.
- **Personality Assessments:** Utilize tools like the Myers-Briggs Type Indicator (MBTI) or StrengthsFinder to gain a deeper understanding of your personality traits and strengths.

## Embrace Your Uniqueness

Authentic living requires embracing your uniqueness. Each person is different, and your differences make you special. Here's how to embrace your uniqueness:

- **Celebrate Your Strengths:** Identify your strengths and leverage them in your daily life. Focus on what you do well rather than dwelling on your weaknesses.
- **Accept Your Flaws:** Nobody is perfect. Accepting your flaws is crucial for self-acceptance. Work on improving, but don't let imperfections define you.
- **Be Honest:** Be truthful about who you are. Honesty builds trust and shows others that you are genuine.

## Living in Harmony with Your Beliefs

To live authentically, your actions must align with your beliefs. Here are some strategies to ensure your life reflects your core values:

## Define Your Values

Identify the principles that are most important to you. These could include honesty, integrity, compassion, and respect. Write them down and reflect on them regularly.

## Set Boundaries

Setting boundaries is essential to protect your values and maintain your integrity. Learn to say no to things that don't align with your beliefs. This might be difficult at first, but it is crucial for authentic living.

## Make Value-Based Decisions

When faced with decisions, consider your values. Ask yourself if the choice aligns with your principles. This approach ensures that your actions are consistent with your beliefs.

## Practice Integrity

Integrity is the cornerstone of authenticity. It means being honest and having strong moral principles. Practice integrity in all aspects of your life, from personal relationships to professional conduct.

## Confidently Expressing Your True Identity

Expressing your true identity with confidence can be challenging but is vital for authentic living. Here are practical tips to help you:

## Build Self-Confidence

Confidence is key to expressing your true self. Here's how to build it:

- **Self-Acceptance:** Accept yourself as you are. Confidence grows from self-acceptance.
- **Positive Affirmations:** Use positive affirmations to reinforce your self-worth.
- **Small Wins:** Celebrate small achievements to boost your confidence gradually.

## Communicate Effectively

Effective communication is crucial for expressing your true identity. Be clear and assertive in your communication. Here are some tips:

- **Be Direct:** Speak clearly and directly. Avoid beating around the bush.
- **Active Listening:** Listen actively to others. This shows respect and fosters open communication.
- **Non-Verbal Cues:** Pay attention to body language. Non-verbal cues can significantly impact how your message is received.

## Surround Yourself with Supportive People

Your environment plays a significant role in your ability to express your true self. Surround yourself with people who support and encourage you. Seek relationships that are based on mutual respect and understanding.

## Overcome Fear of Judgment

Fear of judgment can hinder you from being authentic. Overcoming this fear is essential. Here are some strategies:

- **Focus on Self-Approval:** Prioritize your own approval over others' opinions. Remember that you can't please everyone.
- **Challenge Negative Thoughts:** Identify and challenge negative thoughts that fuel your fear of judgment.
- **Take Risks:** Gradually take risks when expressing your true self. Start small and build up your confidence.

## Practical Exercises for Authentic Living

Here are some practical exercises to help you integrate authenticity into your daily life:

## Daily Reflection

Spend a few minutes each day reflecting on your actions and decisions. Ask yourself if they align with your values and beliefs. This practice fosters self-awareness and accountability.

## Journaling

Maintain a journal to document your thoughts, feelings, and experiences. Journaling can provide insights into your behavior and help you track your progress towards authentic living.

## Value-Based Goal Setting

Set goals that reflect your core values. These goals should be specific, measurable, achievable, relevant, and time-bound (SMART). Aligning your goals with your values ensures that you are working towards a life that is true to who you are.

## Practice Mindfulness

Practice mindfulness to stay present and aware of your thoughts and feelings. Mindfulness helps you connect with your true self and reduces the influence of external pressures.

Living authentically is about knowing yourself, embracing your uniqueness, and aligning your life with your values. It requires courage, honesty, and self-awareness. By following these guidelines, you can live in harmony with your beliefs and confidently express your true identity. Remember, the journey to authenticity is ongoing. It's about making consistent choices that reflect who you truly are. Embrace the journey, and live a life that is authentically yours.

# CHAPTER 11:
## THE ART OF LETTING GO

In life, we often find ourselves caught in a web of emotional and material attachments that can hinder our pursuit of true inner peace. Detachment, contrary to common misconceptions, isn't about abandoning your responsibilities or living a life devoid of joy. It's about finding balance and understanding the transient nature of our possessions and emotions.

## Understanding Emotional Detachment

Emotional detachment doesn't mean you stop caring about others. It means you stop letting their actions and emotions control your mental state. Many people confuse detachment with indifference. However, true emotional detachment is about maintaining your peace and stability regardless of external circumstances.

Imagine you're on a boat in the middle of a turbulent sea. Emotional attachment is like trying to control the waves. Detachment is about learning to navigate your boat through the storm without getting overwhelmed.

## The Impact of Emotional Attachment

Emotional attachment can lead to stress, anxiety, and an overall sense of dissatisfaction. When we tie our happiness to the behavior of others, we give away our power. For example, if your mood is dependent on your partner's actions, you're likely to experience a roller coaster of emotions. This constant fluctuation prevents you from achieving inner peace.

### Practicing Emotional Detachment

1. **Mindfulness:** Being present in the moment helps you to observe your emotions without being consumed by them. When you feel a surge of emotion, take a moment to breathe and acknowledge it without judgment.
2. **Setting Boundaries:** Healthy relationships are built on mutual respect. Setting boundaries ensures that you're not overextending yourself or compromising your well-being.
3. **Self-Awareness:** Understand your triggers and patterns. Self-awareness allows you to respond rather than react to situations.
4. **Acceptance:** Accept that you cannot control others. Focus on what you can control – your reactions and your mindset.

# Material Detachment: Freeing Yourself from the Shackles of Possessions

### The Illusion of Ownership

Material detachment is about recognizing that possessions do not define your worth or happiness. In a consumer-driven society, we're often led to believe that more possessions equate to greater happiness. However, this is an illusion. The more we accumulate, the more we worry about maintaining and protecting our possessions.

### The Burden of Excess

Owning too much can become a burden. The maintenance, storage, and concern over losing these items can lead to significant stress. Moreover, material possessions can create a false sense of security. We start to believe that our happiness and safety are tied to these objects.

### Embracing Minimalism

1. **Decluttering:** Start by assessing your belongings. Ask yourself if each item adds value to your life. If not, consider letting it go. This process can be therapeutic and liberating.

2. **Mindful Consumption:** Before making a purchase, reflect on whether it is a necessity or a fleeting desire. This mindset helps reduce impulsive buying and encourages sustainable living.

3. **Value Experiences Over Things:** Invest in experiences rather than objects. Memories and experiences often bring more lasting joy and fulfillment than material possessions.

4. **Financial Freedom:** Reducing material desires can lead to better financial health. With fewer things to buy and maintain, you can save more and invest in your future.

## The Intersection of Emotional and Material Detachment

Emotional and material detachment are interconnected. When we let go of the need to possess, whether it's emotions or material things, we free ourselves from unnecessary burdens. This doesn't mean we don't care about people or enjoy nice things; it means we understand their place in our lives and don't let them dictate our happiness.

## Achieving Balance

1. **Gratitude:** Practice gratitude for what you have without becoming overly attached. Gratitude shifts your focus from what you lack to what you have, fostering contentment.

2. **Purposeful Living:** Align your actions with your values and goals. When your life is purpose-driven, the need for external validation diminishes.

3. **Inner Peace:** Cultivate inner peace through meditation, self-reflection, and spending time in nature. Inner peace makes it easier to detach from external factors that can disturb your tranquility.

Consider the story of John, a successful entrepreneur who had everything – a thriving business, a luxurious home, and a fancy car. Despite his success, he felt an emptiness that material wealth couldn't fill. John decided to simplify his life. He downsized his home, sold his car, and started focusing on experiences rather than possessions. He also began practicing mindfulness and setting boundaries in his relationships. Over time, John found a sense of peace and fulfillment that he had never experienced before.

On the other hand, Sarah, a social worker, always put others' needs before her own. She often felt drained and unappreciated. By learning to detach emotionally, she started setting boundaries and prioritizing self-care. This shift not only improved her mental health but also made her more effective in her work. Detachment, both emotional and material, is not about isolation or indifference. It's about understanding that true peace comes from within, not from external sources. By practicing mindfulness, setting boundaries, decluttering, and living purposefully, we can achieve a balanced life where our inner peace is no longer at the mercy of external circumstances. Embrace detachment as a tool for a more fulfilling and serene life.

# Personal Stories: Illustrating the Power of Letting Go of Attachments

Understanding the concept of detachment through real-life stories can be incredibly impactful. Here, we explore personal anecdotes of individuals who have embraced emotional and material detachment and the transformative effects it had on their lives.

## John's Journey: From Materialism to Minimalism

### The Initial Struggle

John was a high-flying corporate executive living the quintessential American dream. He owned a sprawling mansion and luxury cars and had an enviable lifestyle. Yet, despite his outward success, John felt a persistent void. His days were filled with stress, his nights with restless sleep. The endless cycle of acquiring more never brought the fulfillment he sought.

### The Turning Point

John's turning point came during a vacation to a remote village in Thailand. He observed the locals, who lived with far less than he had yet radiated contentment and joy. Intrigued by their simple, unburdened lives, John began to question his own materialistic pursuits.

### The Transformation

Inspired by his experience, John decided to simplify his life. He sold his mansion and luxury cars, moved into a modest home, and focused on reducing his possessions to essentials. This process, although challenging, proved liberating. He felt lighter, less stressed, and more in tune with what truly mattered.

### The Positive Impact

John's shift to minimalism led to significant positive changes. Financially, he found himself more secure and less anxious. He invested his savings wisely and pursued passions that brought genuine joy, like painting and volunteering. Emotionally, he became more present and appreciative of his relationships. The void he once felt was replaced with a sense of peace and fulfillment.

# Sarah's Story: Setting Boundaries for Emotional Freedom

### The Overwhelmed Caregiver

Sarah, a dedicated social worker, spent years prioritizing others' needs over her own. Her deep empathy often left her feeling drained and emotionally exhausted. She found it difficult to detach from the pain and struggles of those she helped, carrying their burdens as if they were her own.

### The Wake-Up Call

Sarah's wake-up call came during a health scare. Her doctor advised her to reduce stress or face serious health consequences. Realizing she needed to change, Sarah began exploring ways to manage her emotional attachments.

### The Path to Detachment

Sarah started by practicing mindfulness and meditation, learning to observe her emotions without being overwhelmed. She set clear boundaries at work, ensuring she had time for self-care and personal interests. This was not easy, as it went against her ingrained habits of putting others first. But gradually, she noticed a positive shift in her well-being.

### The Positive Impact

As Sarah learned to detach emotionally, her mental health improved significantly. She became more resilient, less prone to burnout, and more effective in her work.

By setting boundaries, she could offer better support to those in her care without sacrificing her own health. Her personal relationships also thrived as she became more present and attentive, unburdened by constant stress.

# David's Decluttered Life: Finding Joy in Simplicity

### The Cluttered Existence

David, a middle-aged teacher, lived in a house filled with items collected over decades. His attachment to these possessions was rooted in nostalgia and a fear of letting go. However, the clutter created a chaotic environment, adding to his stress and anxiety.

### The Moment of Realization

David's realization came during a particularly stressful school year. Overwhelmed by his surroundings, he decided to declutter his home during the summer break. He began by sorting through his belongings, questioning the value each item brought to his life.

### The Decluttering Process

The process was painstaking. David tackled one room at a time, discarding items that no longer served a purpose. He donated clothes, sold old gadgets, and recycled unnecessary papers. The physical act of decluttering was therapeutic, giving him a sense of control and clarity.

### The Positive Impact

The transformation in David's life was profound. His home became a serene, organized space that promoted relaxation and focus. The reduction in physical clutter mirrored a decrease in mental clutter, making him more efficient and less stressed. He discovered a newfound joy in simplicity and began applying the principles of minimalism to other areas of his life, including his teaching methods.

# Lisa's Emotional Liberation: From Heartbreak to Healing

### The Heartbroken Individual

Lisa, a young professional, experienced a devastating breakup that left her emotionally shattered. Her attachment to her ex-partner made it difficult for her to move on, leading to a cycle of sadness and regret.

### The Path to Healing

Lisa sought therapy, where she learned about emotional detachment. She began practicing techniques to let go of her emotional dependency, such as journaling her feelings, engaging in hobbies, and spending time with supportive friends and family.

### The Journey of Self-Discovery

Through this process, Lisa discovered her own strength and resilience. She started setting personal goals and pursuing activities that brought her joy and fulfillment. Her focus shifted from what she had lost to what she could gain from her experiences.

### The Positive Impact

Lisa's journey of emotional detachment led to profound personal growth. She developed a healthier self-image and stronger emotional resilience. Her relationships with friends and family deepened as she became more present and authentic. Professionally, she excelled, no longer distracted by past regrets. Lisa's story is a testament to the power of emotional detachment in overcoming heartbreak and finding inner peace.

Whether it's reducing material possessions, setting emotional boundaries, or healing from heartbreak, the journey towards detachment leads to greater inner peace and fulfillment.

By letting go of attachments that no longer serve us, we create space for what truly matters, paving the way for a more serene and meaningful life. Embrace detachment not as a loss but as a gain – a step towards a balanced, content, and liberated existence.

# Practical Exercises: Steps to Practice Detachment in Your Own Life

Practicing detachment can significantly enhance your well-being, allowing you to navigate life with greater ease and peace. Here are some practical exercises to help you incorporate emotional and material detachment into your daily routine.

# Emotional Detachment: Techniques to Cultivate Inner Peace

## 1. Mindfulness Meditation

**Steps:**

1. **Find a Quiet Space:** Choose a quiet place where you won't be disturbed.
2. **Sit Comfortably:** Sit in a comfortable position, keeping your back straight.
3. **Focus on Your Breath:** Close your eyes and focus on your breath. Inhale deeply through your nose, hold for a few seconds, and exhale slowly through your mouth.
4. **Observe Your Thoughts:** As thoughts come to your mind, observe them without judgment. Acknowledge their presence and let them pass like clouds in the sky.
5. **Practice Regularly:** Start with 5-10 minutes daily and gradually increase the duration as you become more comfortable with the practice.

## 2. Journaling

**Steps:**

1. **Set Aside Time:** Dedicate a specific time each day for journaling, preferably in the morning or before bed.
2. **Write Freely:** Write about your thoughts, feelings, and experiences without censoring yourself. Focus on how you feel rather than what happened.
3. **Reflect on Patterns:** After a week or two, review your entries to identify any recurring themes or patterns in your thoughts and emotions.
4. **Set Intentions:** Write down your intentions to let go of specific attachments that you've identified.

3. **Setting Boundaries**

**Steps:**

1. **Identify Your Limits:** Reflect on situations or relationships where you feel overextended or uncomfortable.
2. **Communicate Clearly:** Express your boundaries assertively and respectfully. Use "I" statements to convey your needs (e.g., "I need some time for myself in the evenings").
3. **Stick to Your Boundaries:** Consistently enforce your boundaries, even if it feels uncomfortable at first. Remember that maintaining boundaries is essential for your well-being.

4. **Practice Self-Compassion**

**Steps:**

1. **Acknowledge Your Feelings:** Recognize and accept your emotions without judgment.
2. **Speak Kindly to Yourself:** Use positive affirmations and self-talk. Treat yourself with the same kindness you would offer a friend.
3. **Engage in Self-Care:** Participate in activities that nurture your mind, body, and spirit, such as taking a warm bath, reading a book, or going for a walk in nature.

# Material Detachment: Strategies to Simplify Your Life

1. **Decluttering**

**Steps:**

1. **Start Small:** Begin with a small area, such as a drawer or a closet.
2. **Categorize Items:** Sort items into categories: keep, donate, sell, and discard.

3. **Ask Yourself:** For each item, ask if it brings you joy or serves a practical purpose. If not, consider letting it go.

4. **Gradually Expand:** Once you've tackled smaller areas, move on to larger spaces, such as rooms or entire sections of your home.

## 2. Mindful Consumption

**Steps:**

1. **Assess Needs vs. Wants:** Before making a purchase, ask yourself if the item is a necessity or a desire.

2. **Implement a Waiting Period:** Create a rule to wait 24-48 hours before making non-essential purchases. This helps prevent impulse buying.

3. **Reflect on Your Spending:** Regularly review your spending habits and identify areas where you can cut back or make more mindful choices.

## 3. Digital Detox

**Steps:**

1. **Set Boundaries:** Designate specific times of the day when you disconnect from digital devices, such as during meals or before bed.

2. **Unsubscribe:** Unsubscribe from email lists, social media accounts, or apps that don't add value to your life.

3. **Limit Screen Time:** Use apps or built-in features on your devices to track and limit your screen time.

## 4. Value Experiences Over Possessions

**Steps:**

1. **Prioritize Experiences:** Invest in experiences that create lasting memories, such as travel, learning a new skill, or spending time with loved ones.

2. **Create a Budget:** Allocate a portion of your budget for experiences rather than material goods.

3. **Reflect on Happiness:** Keep a journal to note how different experiences make you feel compared to acquiring new possessions.

# Combining Emotional and Material Detachment

## 1. Gratitude Practice

**Steps:**

1. **Daily Gratitude:** Each day, write down three things you're grateful for. Focus on experiences and relationships rather than material items.
2. **Express Thanks:** Share your gratitude with others. Expressing appreciation strengthens relationships and fosters emotional detachment from negative feelings.
3. **Reflect on Abundance:** Regularly review your gratitude entries to remind yourself of the abundance in your life.

## 2. Purposeful Living

**Steps:**

1. **Identify Core Values:** Reflect on what matters most to you. Write down your core values and life goals.

2. **Align Actions:** Make decisions and take actions that align with your core values. This helps reduce the influence of external attachments on your sense of fulfillment.

3. **Regular Check-Ins:** Periodically assess your life to ensure you're living in alignment with your values and making adjustments as needed.

Practicing detachment requires consistent effort and self-awareness. By incorporating these exercises into your daily routine, you can gradually reduce the hold that emotional and material attachments have on your life. Embrace this journey towards detachment as a path to greater inner peace, freedom, and fulfillment.

# CHAPTER 12:
## BUILDING HEALTHY BOUNDARIES

Boundaries are essential to our well-being, yet they are often misunderstood or overlooked. Imagine a world without boundaries—where anyone could walk into your home uninvited, where you were expected to work around the clock without rest, or where your personal space and feelings were constantly disregarded. The chaos, confusion, and stress that would ensue are clear. Boundaries, whether physical, emotional, or psychological, serve as the guardrails of our lives. They help us define who we are, protect our mental health, and ensure that our interactions with others are respectful and balanced.

## Understanding Boundaries

At its core, a boundary is a limit we set to protect our well-being. Boundaries can be physical, like the walls of our home, or emotional, like the limits we set on how others can treat us. They are the lines that distinguish our responsibilities, values, and needs from those of others. Without boundaries, it becomes challenging to maintain a sense of self and preserve our mental health.

Boundaries aren't just about saying "no" to others; they're about saying "yes" to ourselves. By setting limits, we communicate our needs, preferences, and values clearly. This not only helps us protect our mental and emotional health but also fosters healthier relationships. When boundaries are respected, they create a sense of safety and trust, allowing relationships to flourish without resentment or burnout.

# Why Boundaries Matter for Mental Health

### 1. Preserving Emotional Energy

One of the most significant benefits of setting boundaries is the preservation of emotional energy. When we allow others to cross our boundaries—whether by demanding too much of our time, imposing their problems on us, or disrespecting our values—we expend emotional energy that could be better used elsewhere.

Over time, this can lead to feelings of exhaustion, irritability, and burnout. Setting boundaries helps us conserve our emotional resources. It allows us to allocate our time and energy to the things and people that matter most to us, rather than spreading ourselves too thin.

By doing so, we protect our mental health and ensure that we have the emotional bandwidth to take care of ourselves and engage in activities that bring us joy and fulfillment.

### 2. Maintaining a Sense of Identity

Boundaries play a crucial role in maintaining our sense of identity. They help us define who we are, what we stand for, and what we will not tolerate.

Without clear boundaries, we risk losing ourselves in the expectations and demands of others. We may start to prioritize others' needs over our own, leading to a diminished sense of self-worth and identity.

When we set boundaries, we assert our right to be treated with respect and dignity. We communicate to others that our thoughts, feelings, and needs are valid and important. This affirmation of our identity is crucial for maintaining mental health, as it reinforces our self-esteem and self-respect.

### 3. Reducing Anxiety and Stress

Anxiety and stress are often the result of feeling overwhelmed or out of control. When we lack boundaries, we may take on too many responsibilities, say "yes" when we want to say "no," or allow others to encroach on our time and space. This can lead to chronic stress, as we struggle to meet the demands placed on us. Setting boundaries is a powerful tool for reducing anxiety and stress. By clearly defining what we can and cannot do, we create a structure that allows us to manage our responsibilities more effectively. We reduce the likelihood of becoming overwhelmed and ensure that we have the time and space we need to recharge and take care of ourselves.

### 4. Fostering Healthy Relationships

Healthy relationships are built on mutual respect and understanding, both of which are fostered by clear boundaries. When boundaries are established and respected, both parties in a relationship understand each other's needs and limits. This prevents misunderstandings, resentment, and conflicts from arising.

On the other hand, when boundaries are weak or non-existent, relationships can become strained. One person may feel taken advantage of, while the other may feel frustrated by the lack of clear communication. This can lead to a breakdown in trust and respect, ultimately damaging the relationship. By setting and respecting boundaries, we create a foundation of trust and respect that allows relationships to thrive. We ensure that both parties feel valued and heard, leading to deeper and more meaningful connections.

### 5. Empowering Personal Growth

Boundaries are not static; they evolve as we grow and change. By regularly assessing and adjusting our boundaries, we allow ourselves to grow in a way that is aligned with our values and goals. This process of setting and re-evaluating boundaries is empowering, as it gives us control over our lives and our mental health.

When we set boundaries, we take ownership of our well-being. We acknowledge our right to prioritize our needs and take steps to protect our mental health. This sense of agency is crucial for personal growth, as it allows us to make choices that are in line with our values and aspirations.

# How to Set and Maintain Boundaries

Understanding the importance of boundaries is one thing; putting them into practice is another. Setting boundaries can be challenging, especially if we're not used to advocating for ourselves. However, with practice, it becomes easier and more natural.

### 1.  Identify Your Needs and Limits

The first step in setting boundaries is to identify your needs and limits. Take some time to reflect on what is most important to you— your values, priorities, and non-negotiables. Consider the areas of your life where you feel overextended, stressed, or taken for granted. These are likely areas where boundaries need to be established or reinforced.

### 2.  Communicate Clearly and Assertively

Once you've identified your boundaries, the next step is to communicate them clearly and assertively. This doesn't mean being aggressive or confrontational; it simply means being honest and direct about your needs. Use "I" statements to express how you feel and what you need, such as "I need some time alone to recharge" or "I feel uncomfortable when you do that."

### 3.  Be Consistent

Consistency is key to maintaining boundaries. Once you've set a boundary, it's important to stick to it. This reinforces the boundary and helps others understand that you are serious about your needs. If you waver or make exceptions, it can send mixed signals and make it harder to enforce the boundary in the future.

### 4.  Be Prepared for Pushback

Not everyone will be receptive to your boundaries, and that's okay. Some people may push back or try to test your limits. It's important to stand firm and remind yourself that setting boundaries is not about pleasing others; it's about protecting your mental health.

### 5.  Reassess and Adjust as Needed

Boundaries are not set in stone. As you grow and change, your boundaries may need to be adjusted. Regularly reassess your boundaries to ensure they are still serving your needs and protecting your mental health. If something isn't working, don't be afraid to make changes.

Boundaries are essential for maintaining mental health. They help us preserve our emotional energy, maintain our sense of identity, reduce anxiety and stress, foster healthy relationships, and empower personal growth. While setting boundaries can be challenging, it is a crucial skill for protecting our well-being and ensuring that we live a balanced and fulfilling life. By understanding and implementing boundaries, we take an active role in safeguarding our mental health. We create a life that is aligned with our values, priorities, and needs, allowing us to thrive both personally and in our relationships with others.

## Real-Life Examples: Establishing and Maintaining Boundaries

Boundaries are not just theoretical concepts; they are practical tools that real people use every day to protect their mental health and well-being. Here are some real-life examples of how individuals have established and maintained boundaries in various aspects of their lives.

### 1. Oprah Winfrey: Saying "No" to Protect Personal Space

Oprah Winfrey, one of the most influential media personalities in the world, has spoken openly about the importance of boundaries in her life. In an interview with *The New York Times*, Oprah shared how she learned to say "no" as a way to protect her personal space and mental health. In the early days of her career, Oprah found herself overwhelmed by the demands on her time. She was constantly saying "yes" to everything—every event, every request, and every opportunity—because she felt obligated to please others. However, this left her feeling drained and unable to focus on her own needs.

Oprah realized that to preserve her well-being, she needed to set boundaries. She started saying "no" to requests that didn't align with her values or priorities, even if it meant disappointing others. This decision allowed her to focus on what truly mattered to her, such as her own self-care and meaningful projects. Oprah's ability to establish and maintain boundaries has been crucial in sustaining her long-term success and personal fulfillment.

### 2. Brené Brown: Protecting Time for Family

Brené Brown, a renowned research professor and author, is known for her work on vulnerability and courage. Despite her busy schedule as a speaker, writer, and researcher, Brown has been very deliberate about setting boundaries to protect her time with her family.

Brown shared in interviews and her books how she decided to limit her travel and speaking engagements to ensure she could spend more time at home with her husband and children. She recognized that while her career was important, her family was her top priority, and she needed to create boundaries to honor that. By setting limits on her professional commitments, Brown was able to maintain a balance between her work and personal life. She made it clear to her colleagues and clients that her family time was non-negotiable. This boundary allowed her to be fully present with her family, which in turn enriched her personal relationships and contributed to her overall sense of well-being.

### 3.  Michelle Obama: Setting Boundaries in the White House

During her time as First Lady, Michelle Obama was very intentional about setting boundaries to protect her family's privacy and well-being. Living in the White House meant that the Obama family was constantly in the public eye, and there was immense pressure on Michelle to fulfill a wide range of roles and responsibilities.

In her memoir, *Becoming*, Michelle Obama describes how she set boundaries to ensure that her daughters, Malia and Sasha, could have as normal a childhood as possible, despite their unique circumstances. She insisted that the family have regular dinners together, where they could talk and connect without the distractions of their public lives. Michelle also limited the girls' participation in public events and ensured they had time for their schoolwork and hobbies, just like any other children.

These boundaries were crucial in helping the Obama family maintain a sense of normalcy and stability during their time in the White House. By prioritizing her family's needs and setting clear limits on their public exposure, Michelle Obama was able to protect their mental health and well-being.

### 4.  Mark Zuckerberg: Limiting Screen Time

Mark Zuckerberg, co-founder and CEO of Facebook, is another example of someone who has set boundaries to maintain a healthy work-life balance. Despite being at the helm of one of the largest tech companies in the world, Zuckerberg has been vocal about the importance of limiting screen time, both for himself and his family.

Zuckerberg and his wife, Priscilla Chan, have established strict rules around screen time in their household. They limit the amount of time their children spend on devices and are careful about their own screen usage, especially during family time. Zuckerberg has also set personal boundaries around his work schedule, such as taking time off to be with his family after the birth of his children.

These boundaries are particularly significant given Zuckerberg's role in the tech industry, where the lines between work and personal life can easily blur. By setting limits on screen time and prioritizing family time, Zuckerberg demonstrates how even those at the forefront of the digital age can create boundaries to protect their mental health and well-being.

### 5.  Arianna Huffington: Prioritizing Sleep

Arianna Huffington, co-founder of *The Huffington Post* and founder of *Thrive Global*, has been a vocal advocate for the importance of sleep and self-care. After collapsing from exhaustion in 2007, Huffington realized that she needed to set boundaries to prioritize her health. Huffington made sleep a non-negotiable part of her routine, setting a firm boundary around her bedtime. She also implemented a "digital detox" before bed, where she disconnects from her devices to wind down and prepare for a restful night's sleep. This boundary extends to her work culture as well; she encourages her employees to prioritize their well-being and avoid burnout.

Huffington's experience underscores the importance of setting boundaries around self-care. By prioritizing sleep and setting limits on her work and screen time, she was able to recover from burnout and maintain her health, ultimately leading to greater productivity and success in her career.

# Implementing Boundaries: Practical Advice and Techniques

Setting and maintaining boundaries is crucial for protecting your mental health and fostering healthy relationships. However, knowing how to create and uphold boundaries can be challenging, especially if you're not used to advocating for yourself. Here are some practical techniques and advice to help you implement boundaries in your own life.

## 1. Identify Your Needs and Limits

The first step in setting boundaries is to understand your own needs, limits, and values. Reflect on what is most important to you and where you feel your boundaries are currently being crossed. Ask yourself:

- What are my non-negotiables in relationships, work, and personal time?
- Where do I feel most stressed or overwhelmed?
- Are there situations where I consistently feel taken advantage of or disrespected?

Once you have a clear understanding of your needs, you can begin to establish boundaries that protect your well-being.

## 2. Start Small and Be Specific

If setting boundaries is new for you, it's best to start small. Choose one area of your life where you feel a boundary is most needed and focus on that first. For example, you might decide to set a boundary around your availability after work hours or establish a limit on how much time you spend on social media.

When setting a boundary, be as specific as possible. Vague boundaries are harder to enforce and more likely to be misunderstood. Instead of saying, "I need more personal time," you could say, "I will not check work emails after 7 PM." The more specific you are, the easier it will be to uphold your boundary.

### 3. Communicate Clearly and Confidently

Communication is key to implementing boundaries. Once you've identified a boundary, you need to communicate it clearly to those it affects. Use direct and assertive language, but remain respectful and calm. For example:

- "I've decided that I need to focus on my work during the day, so I won't be available for non-work-related calls until after 6 PM."
- "I appreciate your input, but I need to make this decision on my own."

It's important to use "I" statements, which focus on your own needs and feelings rather than blaming or criticizing others. This approach makes it clear that the boundary is about your well-being and is not a personal attack on anyone else.

### 4. Practice Saying "No"

Learning to say "no" is one of the most effective ways to enforce boundaries. Many people struggle with saying "no" because they fear disappointing others or being perceived as uncooperative. However, saying "no" is an essential skill for protecting your time and energy.

When you need to say "no," keep it simple and direct. You don't owe anyone a lengthy explanation. For example:

- "No, I can't take on that extra project right now."
- "No, I'm not available to meet this weekend."

If saying "no" directly feels too difficult at first, you can buy yourself some time by saying, "Let me think about it and get back to you." This allows you to assess whether the request aligns with your boundaries without feeling pressured to respond immediately.

## 5. Use Technology to Your Advantage

Technology can be a powerful tool in setting and maintaining boundaries, especially in today's digital world. Here are a few ways you can use technology to support your boundaries:

- **Set Do Not Disturb**: Most smartphones have a "Do Not Disturb" feature that you can activate during certain hours to prevent notifications from interrupting your personal time.
- **Use Email Filters**: Create filters that sort non-urgent emails into a separate folder, so you're not constantly bombarded with messages that don't require immediate attention.
- **Schedule Breaks**: Use calendar apps to block off time for breaks or personal activities, ensuring that others know you're unavailable during these times.

These small adjustments can help you create a more defined separation between work and personal life, making it easier to maintain your boundaries.

## 6. Be Consistent and Firm

Once you've set a boundary, consistency is key to upholding it. If you allow exceptions too often, others may not take your boundaries seriously, and you might find it harder to enforce them in the future.

Being firm doesn't mean being inflexible. It's okay to reassess and adjust your boundaries as needed, but it's important to remain consistent with the boundaries you've set. For example, if you've decided that weekends are your personal time, don't make exceptions unless it's absolutely necessary. Consistency helps reinforce the boundary and makes it easier for others to respect it.

## 7. Anticipate and Manage Pushback

Not everyone will be happy when you set boundaries, especially if they're used to having unlimited access to your time and energy. You may encounter resistance or pushback from others who don't understand or respect your boundaries.

When this happens, it's important to stay calm and reaffirm your boundary. For example, if a coworker continues to contact you after hours despite your boundary, you could say:

- "I understand that this is important, but as I mentioned, I'm not available after 7 PM. I'll address this first thing in the morning."

Remember, pushback is not a sign that your boundary is wrong. It's a natural reaction from those who are adjusting to the new limits you've set. Stay firm in your decision and give others time to adapt.

## 8. Seek Support if Needed

Setting and maintaining boundaries can be challenging, especially if you're dealing with difficult relationships or a high-pressure environment. Don't hesitate to seek support from trusted friends, family members, or a therapist who can provide guidance and encouragement.

Sometimes, just talking through your boundaries with someone else can give you the confidence you need to enforce them. Additionally, having a support system can help you stay accountable and remind you of the importance of protecting your well-being.

## 9. Reassess and Adjust as Necessary

Boundaries are not static; they should evolve as your needs and circumstances change. Regularly reassess your boundaries to ensure they are still serving you well. Ask yourself:

- Are my boundaries helping me feel more in control and less stressed?
- Do I need to set new boundaries or adjust existing ones?
- Am I consistently upholding my boundaries, or have I let some slip?

If something isn't working, don't be afraid to make changes. Your boundaries should be flexible enough to adapt to new situations but firm enough to protect your core needs.

## 10. Celebrate Your Progress

Finally, remember to celebrate your progress. Setting boundaries is not always easy, especially if it's something you've struggled with in the past. Acknowledge the steps you've taken to protect your well-being and the positive impact it's had on your life. Celebrating your successes, no matter how small, can reinforce the importance of boundaries and motivate you to continue prioritizing your mental health. Implementing boundaries is a vital skill for maintaining mental health and building healthy relationships. By identifying your needs, communicating clearly, staying consistent, and seeking support when needed, you can create boundaries that protect your well-being and help you live a more balanced, fulfilling life. Remember, setting boundaries is an act of self-care, and it's essential for your long-term happiness and success.

# EPILOGUE:
## EMBRACING YOUR IMPERFECTLY PERFECT LIFE

Life is a journey. Each step, each decision, and each experience shapes who we become. For many, this journey is often marred by fear and anxiety. These feelings can be paralyzing, preventing us from achieving our true potential. However, there is a way out.

## Confronting the Fear

In the early stages of this journey, fear was a constant companion. It showed up in various forms: fear of failure, fear of judgment, and fear of the unknown. These fears were paralyzing, preventing any forward momentum. The first step in overcoming fear is acknowledging its presence. You can't fix what you don't see.

I vividly remember my own battles with fear. Every new venture, every public speaking engagement, and every investment decision brought with it a tidal wave of anxiety. My heart would race, my palms would sweat, and my mind would fill with doubts. I realized this fear was rooted in a lack of confidence and a deep-seated belief that I wasn't enough.

## Understanding Anxiety

Anxiety often accompanies fear. It's the lingering doubt that something might go wrong. It's the sleepless nights and the constant worry. Anxiety can be debilitating, but it also offers a clue about what matters most to us. The things we worry about are often the things we care deeply about. For me, anxiety was a daily battle. I worried about my financial future, my career, and my relationships. This constant state of worry took a toll on my health and my overall well-being. I knew I had to find a way to manage this anxiety if I wanted to live a fulfilling life.

## The Turning Point

The turning point came when I realized that fear and anxiety are not enemies to be vanquished but signals to be understood. They are indicators of areas in our lives that require attention and growth. This shift in perspective was crucial. Instead of fighting against fear and anxiety, I began to see them as guides.

I started by asking myself tough questions: Why am I afraid? What is the worst that could happen? How likely is that outcome? This process of questioning helped me to demystify my fears and see them for what they were – often exaggerated and unfounded worries.

## Embracing Change

Change is inevitable, but it's also the source of much of our fear and anxiety. Embracing change rather than resisting it is a powerful step towards transformation. This involves accepting that uncertainty is a part of life and that growth often comes from stepping outside of our comfort zones.

I embraced change by taking calculated risks. I invested in new ventures, spoke at events despite my fears, and made decisions that pushed me beyond my comfort zone. Each step, no matter how small, was a victory over fear.

## Building Confidence

Confidence is the antidote to fear. It comes from taking action and achieving small wins. These victories build upon each other, creating a foundation of self-assurance that can withstand future challenges. One of the most effective ways I built confidence was through continuous learning. I read books, attended seminars, and sought mentorship. Knowledge is empowering; the more I learned, the more confident I became in my abilities.

## Practicing Self-Compassion

Self-compassion is about treating yourself with the same kindness and understanding that you would offer a friend. It's recognizing that everyone makes mistakes and that failure is a part of the journey. This mindset shift was crucial for me. I learned to forgive myself for past mistakes and to view failures as learning opportunities. This self-compassion allowed me to move forward without the heavy burden of self-criticism. It was liberating and paved the way for greater self-acceptance.

## Achieving Serenity

Serenity is not the absence of challenges but the ability to remain calm and focused amidst them. It's the result of managing fear and anxiety effectively and cultivating a sense of inner peace. Achieving serenity involves incorporating mindfulness and meditation into my daily routine. These practices helped me stay present and let go of worries about the future or regrets about the past. They provided a sense of grounding and clarity that was essential for my well-being.

## Self-Acceptance

Self-acceptance is the culmination of this journey. It's about embracing who you are, flaws and all. It's about recognizing and being at peace with your strengths and weaknesses. This doesn't mean complacency but rather a realistic and compassionate view of oneself.

I reached self-acceptance by continuously reflecting on my values and aligning my actions with them. I accepted that perfection is an illusion and that I am a work in progress. This acceptance brought a profound sense of peace and fulfillment.

## Practical Steps to Transform Fear into Serenity

1. **Acknowledge Your Fears:** Write them down and understand their root causes.
2. **Question Your Anxiety:** Analyze the likelihood of your worries coming true.
3. **Embrace Change:** Step out of your comfort zone regularly.
4. **Build Confidence:** Focus on small wins and continuous learning.
5. **Practice Self-Compassion:** Treat yourself with kindness and forgiveness.
6. **Cultivate Mindfulness:** Incorporate meditation or mindfulness practices into your routine.
7. **Reflect and Align:** Regularly assess your values and ensure your actions are in harmony with them.

The journey from fear and anxiety to serenity and self-acceptance is not a straight path but a winding road filled with lessons and growth opportunities. It requires a shift in perspective, embracing change, building confidence, practicing self-compassion, and cultivating mindfulness. By taking these steps, you can transform your life and achieve a state of inner peace and self-acceptance. This transformation is not about becoming someone else but about becoming the best version of yourself. It's about recognizing your worth, facing your fears, and living a life aligned with your values. It's a journey worth taking.

In life, persistence is the cornerstone of growth. Many people start with grand ambitions, yet few see them through to the end. What separates those who succeed from those who don't? It's not always intelligence or talent; often, it's the simple act of not giving up. This lesson is crucial in every aspect of life, from personal development to financial success.

Persistence means pushing forward even when the path gets tough. It means facing obstacles head-on and finding ways around them. It's about maintaining a clear vision of your goals and taking steady, consistent steps towards achieving them. Remember, the journey is as important as the destination. Each challenge you overcome strengthens your resolve and brings you one step closer to your goals.

## Growth Through Challenges

Growth doesn't come from staying within your comfort zone. True growth occurs when you stretch your limits when you dare to venture into the unknown. Embrace challenges as opportunities for growth. Each difficulty you face is a chance to learn, to become stronger, and to develop skills that will serve you in the future. Consider challenges as part of your personal and professional development. Every setback is a lesson in disguise, and every failure is a stepping stone to success. Approach each challenge with a mindset of learning and improvement. This way, you transform potential roadblocks into valuable experiences that contribute to your overall growth.

## The Importance of Self-Compassion

As you pursue your goals, it's essential to practice self-compassion. This means being kind to yourself, especially during times of failure or disappointment. Too often, we are our harshest critics. We hold ourselves to unrealistic standards and punish ourselves when we fall short. This mindset can be detrimental to your growth and well-being.

Self-compassion involves recognizing your humanity and understanding that everyone makes mistakes. It's about treating yourself with the same kindness and understanding that you would offer a friend. When you practice self-compassion, you create a positive environment for growth. You allow yourself the space to learn from your mistakes without the burden of self-judgment.

## Authenticity in Pursuit of Success

Success is not just about achieving financial wealth or professional accolades; it's about being true to yourself. Authenticity means living in alignment with your values and beliefs. It involves understanding who you are, what you stand for, and what you want out of life. When you pursue your goals authentically, you find fulfillment and satisfaction. Being authentic requires self-awareness and honesty. Take the time to reflect on your values and aspirations. Make decisions that align with your true self rather than trying to meet external expectations or societal norms. When you are authentic, your actions are more meaningful, and your success feels more rewarding.

## Embracing Your Unique Journey

Every person's journey is unique. We all have different backgrounds, experiences, and challenges. Embrace your journey and celebrate your individuality. Your path may not look like anyone else's, and that's okay. In fact, that's something to be proud of. Your unique experiences shape who you are and contribute to your growth.

Don't compare your journey to others. Instead, focus on your progress and celebrate your achievements, no matter how small they may seem. Each step forward is a testament to your strength and determination. By embracing your unique journey, you cultivate a sense of pride and satisfaction in your accomplishments.

## Parting Words of Wisdom

As you continue on your path, remember these key principles: persistence, growth, self-compassion, authenticity, and embracing your unique journey. These elements are the foundation of a fulfilling life. They guide you through challenges and help you find meaning and purpose in your endeavors. Life is not a race to the finish line; it's a continuous journey of growth and discovery. Embrace each moment, learn from every experience, and remain true to yourself. Celebrate your achievements and be kind to yourself during setbacks. Your journey is uniquely yours, and it is something to be celebrated.

In the end, leading a fulfilling life means accepting and celebrating who you are. It's about understanding that external achievements do not determine your worth but by your character and integrity. Live authentically, pursue your passions, and persist through challenges. By doing so, you create a life that is rich in meaning and fulfillment.

Remember, the journey is the destination. Each step you take is a part of your unique story. Embrace it with open arms, and you will find that true success lies in the continuous pursuit of growth, self-compassion, and authenticity.

# ABOUT THE AUTHOR

Christopher Gary is an accomplished content creator and author whose passion for storytelling has taken readers on captivating journeys through the pages of his latest novel. With a unique ability to weave intricate plots and breathe life into diverse characters, Christopher has penned this book, pushing the boundaries of the norm.

Born and raised in Kingston, Jamaica, Christopher draws inspiration from his rich cultural background and experiences, infusing authenticity into his narratives. He holds a degree in Business Science and Arts and has honed his craft through years of dedicated writing. Christopher's writing style has been praised for its lyrical prose, compelling dialogue, and skillful balance of tension and emotion.

When Christopher is not immersed in the world of words, he is found watching his Philadelphia sports teams and the Jamaican Olympic teams or spending time with his wife and son, Annette, and CJ. His commitment to family is reflected in his work, adding depth and truth to every story he tells. His latest literary endeavor showcases his continued dedication to crafting stories that resonate with readers across the globe.